A Practical Guide For Parents To Keep Kids Safe Online

DR STEVEN SAM

Copyright © 2024 Steven Sam

All rights reserved.

ISBN: 9798301997709

DISCLAIMER NOTICE

This book serves as a guide for parents, teachers, and caregivers to promote safe and responsible digital habits for children. It is based on widely accepted best practices, expert advice, and reliable sources but is not a replacement for personalised professional guidance. Readers are encouraged to tailor strategies to their family's specific needs and the ever-changing digital environment. The author is not responsible for decisions made using the information provided.

CONTENTS

THE FOUNDATION OF OPEN COMMUNICATION 1
SETTING CLEAR AND EFFECTIVE GUIDELINES 13
MASTERING PARENTAL CONTROLS SETTINGS 25
MONITORING ONLINE ACTIVITY 39
TEACHING DIGITAL CITIZENSHIP 53
ENCOURAGING CRITICAL THINKING ONLINE 67
STAYING CURRENT IN THE DIGITAL WORLD 81
CONCLUSION 96
SUMMARY AND KEY POINTS 98

THE FOUNDATION OF OPEN COMMUNICATION

In today's digital age world, children are exposed to a vast amount of online content, some of which may not always be appropriate or safe. To protect them effectively, creating a safe space for open dialogue between parents and children is important. Communication isn't just a skill—it's a foundational tool for building trust, which becomes the foundation of a child's safety, both online and offline.

Why Open Communication Matters

When children know they can approach their parents without fear of judgment or criticism, they're more likely to share experiences that make them feel uncomfortable. This openness is vital because children often come across content, conversations, or websites that may seem harmless but could expose them to risks they're not prepared to handle alone. Teaching children that they can talk freely without the fear of getting in trouble reinforces their sense of security and confidence in the guidance their parents provide.

Imagine Sarah, a mother of a 10-year-old daughter, Mia. Sarah regularly takes the time to talk to Mia about her online experiences, asking questions like, "What kind of videos do you like watching?" or "Did anything surprise you online today?" These conversations help Mia feel comfortable sharing any online interaction, positive or negative, without hesitation. So, when Mia come across a YouTube video that made her feel uncomfortable, she didn't think twice about telling her mom. They discussed why the video wasn't suitable for her, and Sarah took steps to add filters to Mia's account, ensuring future experiences would be safer. This open line of communication allowed Mia to voice her discomfort confidently, knowing her mom would listen and act

A parent and child in a casual setting having an open conversation

Starting the Conversation

Creating this safe, open environment doesn't have to be complex or daunting. It begins with genuine curiosity about a child's day-to-day experiences, especially online. Many parents hesitate, fearing that asking too many questions may make their child feel like they're being watched or judged. However, focusing on non-intrusive questions that express interest rather than scrutiny can set a comfortable tone. Questions like "What's something new you learned online today?" or "Did anything funny happen online with your friends?" show a natural interest in their world. This approach helps children feel understood, encouraging them to open up when something disturbing happens.

Encouraging a Culture of Sharing

Creating a home environment where children feel comfortable discussing their digital interactions requires consistency and openness from parents. When parents actively foster a culture of sharing, it gradually becomes second nature for kids to communicate freely, even about topics that might feel sensitive or confusing. A practical way to encourage this culture is through daily check-ins that go beyond the typical "How was your day?" Instead, focusing specifically on online experiences helps normalise discussions about their digital lives.

For instance, using phrases like, "Did you see anything interesting online today?" or "What apps did you enjoy using?" can prompt children to open up about their online communications without feeling monitored. It's beneficial to ask about their interests in a way that shows curiosity rather than control. Over time, these questions build a habit of sharing, making it natural for them to speak up when something unusual or concerning occurs.

Carlos, a father of two boys aged 9 and 13, holds daily check-ins, asking, "Anything fun or different online today?" This simple routine fosters open communication about their online experiences. Recently, his older son mentioned a website making exaggerated claims about a "miracle cure." Carlos used this as a teaching moment, guiding his son to research the site's credibility, reinforcing critical thinking. By keeping these check-ins low-pressure, Carlos has created a safe space for his sons to share their digital encounters openly.

Active Listening as a Foundation for Trust

When children share their experiences, particularly those involving online content, it's crucial that parents practice active listening. This means giving children the time and space to express themselves without interruptions, judgments, or immediate solutions. Instead, parents should focus on understanding their child's perspective and emotions, providing a supportive environment. Active listening conveys respect and empathy, making children more motivated to share their thoughts openly.

A parent actively listening to a child share their experiences

For example, consider Emma, a single mother, whose 8-year-old son is an avid tablet user. Emma noticed he had started mentioning certain videos and games that his friends were discussing at school. Instead of immediately setting limits, she listened carefully, asking follow-up questions that helped her understand what he found appealing in these games and videos. She used this opportunity to discuss both fun and safety aspects of online content, ensuring he felt heard while she guided him on making safer choices. Emma's approach demonstrates how active listening can open doors to meaningful conversations, giving children a sense of validation and confidence.

Building a Relationship of Openness and Trust

Building trust takes time and patience. To help children feel secure enough to share both positive and negative experiences, parents can make it clear that they are there to support and protect, not punish. When children know that their honesty won't lead to restrictions or punishment, they are more likely to come forward when they face something potentially harmful online. Reinforcing the idea that safety is the primary goal—not punishment—helps them view their parents as allies rather than enforcers.

As children grow older and become more independent online, this foundation of trust is even more vital. For example, setting clear expectations at the outset about online behaviour and letting children know that they can discuss any issues openly helps prevent secrecy or hesitation. Establishing this trust early can be crucial as children navigate the increasingly complex digital world.

Guiding Conversations About Potential Online Dangers

While keeping communication open is essential, it's equally important for parents to proactively discuss the potential dangers children might encounter online. These discussions should be framed thoughtfully, aiming to inform rather than instil fear. Educating children on these risks helps equip them with the knowledge to navigate the online world safely. Instead of waiting for an issue to arise, regular conversations about online threats like cyberbullying, privacy risks, and inappropriate content can prepare children to recognise and respond to these situations if they occur.

One effective approach is using "What if..." scenarios. These hypothetical situations encourage children to think critically about how they might respond in various circumstances. For instance, a parent could ask, "What if someone you don't know tries to chat with you in a game?" or "What would you do if you saw something online that made you feel uncomfortable?" Questions like these open the floor for discussion, allowing children to explore possible actions and solutions with their parents' guidance.

Consider Monica, a mother of a 12-year-old girl named Sophie. Monica frequently uses these "What if…" questions to prepare Sophie for potentially risky situations online. Recently, Sophie encountered an unfamiliar message in one of her apps, and she instantly remembered their conversations. Knowing exactly what to do, Sophie told her mother, and together, they blocked the user and reported the incident. Monica's strategy of discussing hypothetical scenarios empowered Sophie to act responsibly without feeling panicked or unprepared.

Addressing Cyberbullying and Negative Interactions

Cyberbullying is a particularly sensitive topic, but one that's critical to address early on. Many children, even those in younger age groups, encounter some form of cyberbullying through social media, games, or group chats. Educating children on recognising and handling cyberbullying is a vital aspect of online safety. It's essential to convey that they are not alone, and that seeking help is both appropriate and encouraged.

To approach this topic effectively, parents can discuss how to handle hurtful comments or messages, emphasising that they have the right to block, report, or ignore negative behaviour online. In addition, parents can explain the concept of empathy, helping children understand why hurtful actions can stem from others' insecurities or misunderstandings. This balanced approach helps children recognise the importance of protecting their well-being without responding aggressively.

Take Lisa, whose 13-year-old daughter recently received a hurtful comment on her Instagram post. Instead of brushing it off, Lisa saw this as an opportunity to discuss the impact of cyberbullying and the options available to her daughter. Together, they reported the comment, blocked the user, and talked about ways to cope with online negativity. Lisa's calm and supportive response not only provided her daughter with immediate relief but also empowered her with the tools to handle similar situations independently in the future.

Creating a Judgment-Free Environment

Children need to feel assured that they won't face judgment or shame for anything they might encounter online, especially when they're unsure of what is appropriate. Setting this tone of non-judgment is essential to building a foundation of trust. For instance, if a child accidentally encounters inappropriate content, they should feel confident in approaching their parents without the fear of being criticised. By creating a judgment-free zone, parents ensure their children can turn to them first for support, regardless of the situation.

Reassurance is key in this approach. When parents convey that mistakes happen and that seeking help is always the right step, children are more likely to be open and honest. It's helpful to occasionally remind children that while the internet can be an amazing resource, there are also risks, and their safety is the primary focus.

Using Shared Digital Experiences to Strengthen Communication

One powerful way to reinforce open communication is through shared digital experiences. When parents and children explore the digital world together, it not only builds trust but also creates opportunities for natural conversations about online safety. By joining in these activities, parents gain a first-hand understanding of their children's interests, which makes discussions about online content, games, and interactions feel more relevant and authentic.

For instance, parents can occasionally watch videos, play games, or explore apps with their children. These shared moments provide an open platform for talking about what's appropriate online, helping children feel that their parents are genuinely interested in their digital interests. This approach nurtures a deeper bond and promotes a collaborative approach to safety rather than a top-down set of rules. Engaging with children on their terms shows them that parents respect their digital experiences, strengthening a positive, open communication dynamic.

Consider Nathan, who takes the time to play an online game with his

10-year-old son once a week. Through these sessions, Nathan has become more familiar with the gaming platform, including its chat features and privacy settings. This knowledge has allowed Nathan to naturally integrate safety reminders during gameplay, such as only accepting friend requests from known players. His son appreciates the attention and feels comfortable discussing the game's social aspects with his dad, knowing Nathan understands the game's environment. Nathan's willingness to engage in his son's digital world has laid a solid foundation of trust and openness.

A parent and child working together on a tablet, blocking or reporting inappropriate

Creating "Tech-Free" Family Time to Balance Digital Interactions

While engaging in digital activities together can strengthen communication, creating "tech-free" family moments is equally essential. These offline moments provide a chance to reconnect without screens, helping to create balance and avoid the feeling that digital life dominates everything. Establishing tech-free zones or times—like during family meals, game nights, or outdoor activities—gives everyone a break from devices and encourages deeper, distraction-free conversations.

For example, the simple rule of "no screens at the dinner table" can encourage quality family time. This period of uninterrupted conversation offers a chance to discuss the day's events, including any interesting online experiences or concerns. Over time, tech-free family time strengthens the idea that while digital interactions are a part of life, they shouldn't replace in-person connections. It subtly conveys the message that the family is always present to support one another, both online and offline.

Take Laura and her family, who established a rule of no phones or tablets during evening dinners. By maintaining this consistent practice, Laura created a space where her children naturally open up about their days, including their online experiences. Her teenage daughter recently shared a story about a funny meme from social media, which led to a discussion about online humour, boundaries, and respect. This simple rule has allowed Laura to stay connected with her kids' online lives while preserving meaningful family time, blending both online and offline worlds harmoniously.

Encouraging Openness Through Mutual Respect

Mutual respect forms the core of an open and trusting relationship. When children feel their parents respect their views, they're more likely to return that respect by listening to their parents' guidance. While rules are necessary, involving children in the creation of these rules can further their understanding of online safety and make them feel valued in the process. For example, rather than imposing restrictions alone, parents can sit down with their children to discuss online rules together. This collaborative approach enables children to voice their opinions, ask questions, and understand the reasoning behind each rule. When children are included in these decisions, they're more likely to follow guidelines willingly because they recognise their value and feel a sense of ownership.

Ellie, a mother of two, practiced this approach with her 14-year-old son. Rather than just limiting his screen time, Ellie invited him to discuss what he thought was a fair amount of daily online time. Together, they agreed on rules that balanced his gaming interests with other activities. This collaboration not only set clear boundaries but also made her son more willing to respect and follow the agreed-upon limits. By nurturing mutual respect and engaging her son in decision-making, Ellie created a positive, open environment that reinforced both communication and accountability.

Setting Boundaries on Online Content While Keeping Communication Open

Setting boundaries around online content is an essential component of online safety, but it's also important to ensure these boundaries don't feel restrictive or isolating to children. Clear, age-appropriate guidelines help children understand what's safe to explore online, but they work best when presented as part of a collaborative and open discussion. By framing boundaries as safety measures rather than limitations, parents can create a sense of mutual understanding and collaboration, encouraging children to follow these rents can begin by explaining why certain types of content may not be suitable and discussing how they plan to help manage what children can access. For instance, letting children know that some websites, videos, or apps might expose them to inappropriate or unsafe material makes them more aware of potential dangers. Parents can then stress that these boundaries are not about limiting fun but about ensuring a safe and positive online experience.

Maintaining Flexibility as Kids Grow

As children age, their online interests evolve, and the content they can safely access changes. Maintaining a flexible approach allows parents to adjust boundaries in response to their children's growing maturity, knowledge, and ability to handle online risks. By revisiting these guidelines regularly, parents can ensure they remain relevant and practical, encouraging children to continue practicing safe online habits as they grow.

A great way to include flexibility is through regular "check-ins" where parents and children can openly discuss how current boundaries are working. During these check-ins, parents can ask questions like, "Is there anything new online that you're interested in exploring?" or "Are there any restrictions that you feel we could adjust now?" These conversations signal to children that their voice matters, making them more likely to come forward with any concerns or desires to explore new types of content.

Consider John, who has a 12-year-old son, Alex, with a keen interest in online games. Initially, John had set a rule allowing Alex only one hour of game time each evening. As Alex matured and showed responsibility in balancing his screen time with other activities, they discussed adjusting this limit to include weekends. John also used this opportunity to review the content of Alex's games, ensuring they remained age-appropriate. By keeping an open line of communication and showing a willingness to adapt the rules, John helped Alex feel respected and trusted, fostering an ongoing dialogue about safety and responsibility.

Communicating Safety as a Shared Responsibility

Another key element in setting boundaries is framing online safety as a shared responsibility between parent and child. Children should understand that their parents are there to support and protect them, but that they also have a role in staying safe by making responsible choices. By inspiring children to take part in their own safety, parents can nurture a sense of independence and responsibility. One effective way to encourage shared responsibility is by teaching children when it is important to seek help. For instance, encouraging children to tell a parent if they come across something unfamiliar or uncomfortable online builds their confidence in exploring digital spaces safely. Supporting the idea that they're part of a "safety team" promotes the understanding that online safety is not just about rules but about mutual respect and protection.

Carlos, a father of two, regularly reminds his children that they're a part of the family's "online safety team." By instilling a sense of shared responsibility, he has helped his children understand that they play an active role in protecting themselves online. Recently, when his teenage son came across an unfamiliar pop-up on a gaming site, he knew to tell Carlos about it right away. Carlos's approach not only strengthened the boundaries they had set but also encouraged his son to be proactive in maintaining his own safety.

SETTING CLEAR AND EFFECTIVE GUIDELINES

In a world where screens are nearly everywhere, establishing clear guidelines around device use has become essential for children's well-being. Setting boundaries on when and how digital devices can be used helps children develop a balanced relationship with technology, inspiring them to enjoy its benefits while also appreciating offline experiences. Effective guidelines are neither rigid rules nor random restrictions—they're tools for creating a sustainable structure that nurtures healthy habits and independence.

Why Structure is Important for Children

Children do well with routine, feeling safe and comfortable in a structured environment. Consistent rules around device use provide this structure, helping them learn to manage their time and focus on a variety of activities. Setting boundaries helps parents communicate expectations, guiding children toward responsible online behaviour and preventing them from getting too absorbed in digital content. This balance is crucial not only for maintaining family harmony but also for encouraging children to engage in offline interests and social activities, which contribute to their overall development.

John, a father of 12-year-old Alex, noticed his son spending hours immersed in video games. To create balance, John introduced a new rule: no video games after 7 p.m. Instead, the family used this time to play board games or read together. This simple guideline helped shift Alex's focus to other meaningful activities without taking away something he enjoyed. It also strengthened the importance of balancing online fun with offline moments.

A parent and child setting screen time guidelines together

Setting Guidelines Together

Involving children in the process of setting these boundaries can lead to smoother adherence and promote mutual respect. When children feel they have a say in the rules, they are more likely to understand and accept them. This shared approach also teaches them the value of compromise and helps them develop critical thinking skills as they weigh the benefits and potential problems of screen time.

For instance, parents might sit down with their children and explain the reasons behind each guideline, such as how excessive screen time can affect sleep or make it harder to concentrate in school. By providing explanations and inviting children to share their thoughts, parents show respect for their perspectives. This process not only strengthens the parent-child bond but also gives children a sense of ownership over the rules, making it easier for them to follow the agreed-upon guidelines.

Structuring Screen Time for Balance

One of the most effective ways to manage screen time is to establish a daily or weekly schedule that balances online and offline activities. By setting specific time blocks for screen use, children can enjoy their digital interests while also dedicating time to schoolwork, physical activities, and family interactions. This approach to time management helps children develop a sense of responsibility over their daily routines and learn to prioritise tasks, a skill that will serve them well throughout their lives.

A popular guideline many families adopt is the "30-60-10" rule, which suggests that for every 30 minutes of screen time, children should engage in at least 10 minutes of a physical activity or an offline activity, such as reading or drawing. This method helps break up prolonged periods of screen use, preventing children from becoming too engaged in digital media and encouraging regular movement. These short breaks are especially important for younger children, as they can help reduce eye strain and maintain attention levels.

Consider Carlos, a father of three children ages 6, 10, and 14. Carlos introduced a "30-60-10" rule for their screen time, and together they created a family calendar where each child's preferred activities are marked. For every hour they spend playing online games or watching videos, they rotate through offline activities like helping with cooking, playing sports, or spending time outdoors. Carlos's children have embraced the structure, finding enjoyment in both digital and offline experiences. This approach has not only kept their screen time in check but also fostered family unity as they share quality offline moments together.

Creating "Device-Free Zones" at Home

Another strategy that helps maintain a healthy relationship with technology is designating "device-free zones" within the home. These are areas where screens aren't allowed, such as the dinner table, family room, or bedrooms. Having designated screen-free spaces helps children associate these areas with offline activities, encouraging them to engage with family members, focus on schoolwork, or unwind without the distraction of devices. By establishing these zones, parents can help children understand that while devices are useful, they don't belong everywhere, setting a foundation for balanced usage.

A "device-free" dinner table with family members engaging in conversation.

For instance, Emma, a single mother, noticed her son Noah bringing his tablet to the dinner table, causing distractions during meals. She introduced a new rule: no devices at the dinner table. To ease the transition, Emma encouraged Noah to share stories and talk about his day during dinner. Over time, Noah adjusted to the "device-free" rule and began enjoying family time without the tablet. Emma's approach helped Noah appreciate the importance of being present and respecting moments free from digital distractions.

Balancing Online Activities with Offline Hobbies

Encouraging children to pursue offline hobbies is another way to balance screen time. When children have hobbies they enjoy, such as playing a musical instrument, drawing, or engaging in sports, they're less likely to depend on screens for entertainment. Offline interests not only provide an alternative to screen-based activities but also help children develop valuable skills and build confidence. Parents can support their children in discovering and nurturing these interests, whether by enrolling them in classes, joining them in activities, or simply making space in their schedules for these pursuits.

Take Laura and her teenage daughter, Clara. Clara loves spending time online but also has a passion for drawing. Laura has supported this interest by setting up a small art space in Clara's room and encouraging her to spend time there each day. With her mother's encouragement, Clara now balances her screen time with her drawing sessions, finding joy in both pursuits. By fostering this interest, Laura has helped Clara cultivate a fulfilling offline activity that gives her a break from screens and adds a creative outlet to her daily routine

Managing Content Access with Clear Boundaries

When it comes to online content, children need guidance on what is safe and appropriate for their age group. Establishing clear boundaries around the types of content they can access helps protect them from potentially harmful material while also teaching them responsible digital habits. Parents can set these boundaries by enabling parental controls on devices and streaming services, creating age-appropriate profiles, and regularly reviewing the types of content that align with their family's values.

Using tools like YouTube Kids, Google SafeSearch, or specific content filters available on streaming platforms provides parents with options to manage what their children can access. However, it's essential to involve children in conversations about why certain boundaries exist, helping them understand the reasons behind these limitations. This dialogue can make the boundaries feel less like restrictions and more like protective measures that prioritise their safety.

Olivia, for instance, is a mother of an 8-year-old boy, Liam. She has enabled parental controls on his tablet and set up a YouTube Kids account for safe browsing. When setting up these restrictions, Olivia explained to Liam that some content isn't suitable for his age because it might contain language or ideas he wouldn't fully understand. By approaching the topic with honesty and respect, Olivia helped Liam see the controls as part of their family's safety plan, making it easier for him to accept them without resistance.

Promoting Responsibility with Age-Appropriate Rules

As children grow older, they naturally become more curious and independent in their online activities. Tailoring rules to their age and maturity level helps build their sense of responsibility while ensuring they remain safe. For younger children, stricter controls and more supervision may be necessary, while pre-teens and teenagers can gradually be given more freedom within established guidelines. This approach reinforces trust and responsibility, showing children that their actions influence the level of freedom they're granted.

For example, Carlos and his teenage daughter, Sofia, have developed a rule: she can access social media platforms under the condition that her parents review her profiles together once a month. This arrangement has allowed Sofia to enjoy connecting with her friends online while also providing her parents with peace of mind. As Sofia has demonstrated responsibility by following family guidelines and practicing online safety, Carlos has gradually loosened some restrictions, rewarding her trustworthiness. This balanced approach enables Sofia to manage her online interactions independently, while still ensuring her parents' involvement for safety.

Encouraging Transparency and Openness

In addition to rules and restrictions, maintaining an environment of openness is crucial for content management. When children feel they can openly discuss their online interests or concerns, they are more likely to reach out when they encounter something unsettling or confusing. Building this trust requires parents to be non-judgmental and receptive, creating a safe space where children can talk about their experiences without fear of criticism.

A parent and child reviewing online content settings together on a tablet or laptop.

Consider Monica, whose 10-year-old son, Jake, recently discovered a popular video game that many of his classmates play. When he asked if he could try it, Monica sat down with Jake and reviewed the game together, explaining what she felt was appropriate and what wasn't. She set specific rules, such as no chatting with strangers, and explained that her goal was to keep him safe, not to take away his enjoyment. By approaching the conversation openly, Monica showed Jake that she respected his interests while prioritising his safety, encouraging him to come to her with future requests.

Creating a Family Media Plan

A family media plan can be a powerful tool for setting clear expectations around device usage and online behaviour. This plan serves as a collective agreement, allowing each family member to understand their roles, responsibilities, and boundaries regarding screen time and digital interactions. By developing a family media plan together, parents and children can agree on goals, making it easier for everyone to respect and follow the guidelines.

To create an effective plan, parents can start by listing the most important aspects they want to cover, such as screen time limits, device-free zones, content restrictions, and time for family activities. Each section should be age-appropriate and adapted to individual family needs. Additionally, the plan can include rewards for following the rules consistently, like extra screen time on weekends, which can motivate children to adhere to the guidelines.

Consider the example of Laura and her two children, ages 8 and 14. To address their different needs, Laura created a media plan that specified unique guidelines for each child. For her younger child, screen time was limited to one hour per day, and all games had to be age appropriate. For her older teenager, Laura agreed to a more flexible plan, including two hours of screen time each day with the understanding that homework and chores must come first. By accommodating each child's needs, Laura created a balanced plan that provided structure and flexibility, encouraging a sense of fairness and mutual respect.

A PRACTICAL GUIDE FOR PARENTS TO KEEP KIDS SAFE ONLINE

Family discussing a media plan around a table with a calendar

Setting Boundaries for "Work" vs. "Leisure" Screen Time

Not all screen time is created equal. Children often use devices for various purposes, including educational activities, schoolwork, and entertainment. Differentiating between "work" and "leisure" screen time can help parents set more realistic expectations around device use, ensuring that children focus on educational content while still having room for entertainment.

For example, many families implement a rule that screens used for schoolwork or creative projects do not count toward daily screen time limits. This rule allows children to complete assignments or explore hobbies without the pressure of counting minutes, while still enforcing limits on purely recreational screen use. By separating productive and recreational activities, families can encourage responsible device use that encourages learning and creativity.

John, a father of a 13-year-old daughter, has established this distinction in their family media plan. His daughter can use her laptop for school projects without it counting against her daily screen time. However, recreational activities, like watching movies or playing games, are limited to 90 minutes a day. John's approach teaches his daughter that screens can serve different purposes and helps her make conscious choices about how she spends her time online.

Reviewing and Adjusting the Plan as Needed

A family media plan should be flexible, evolving as children grow and their digital needs change. Periodically reviewing and adjusting the plan keeps it relevant and ensures that it continues to support the family's goals and values. Parents can schedule family meetings every few months to discuss how the plan is working, what needs improvement, and if any adjustments are necessary. This process enables children to participate actively in shaping their digital environment, strengthening a sense of responsibility and collaboration.

For instance, Carlos and his family hold a family meeting every three months to review their media plan. During these meetings, each family member shares their thoughts on what's working and any challenges they've encountered. Recently, Carlos's teenage son expressed a desire to extend his weekend screen time by one hour. After discussing the reasons and setting expectations, the family agreed to adjust the plan. This collaborative process has made the family media plan adaptable and sustainable, giving each family member a voice while maintaining a balanced approach to screen use.

Managing Devices with Consistency

Consistency is the key to making any family media plan work effectively. Once boundaries and guidelines are in place, sticking to them helps children understand that screen time rules aren't negotiable or situational but are part of their daily routine. By consistently applying rules across all devices and situations, parents strengthen the importance of responsible screen use and prevent confusion around expectations.

One way to maintain consistency is by using device management tools that apply time limits and content filters automatically. Many devices now have built-in features that allow parents to set time limits and monitor usage, making it easier to enforce guidelines without constantly intervening. For example, setting up automatic downtime on devices at certain hours, like bedtime or during family meals, helps reinforce device-free periods and reduces the need for reminders.

Amelia a mother of three, uses parental controls to set consistent screen time limits for each of her children. Each device is configured with specific limits that align with their family media plan, such as an hour of recreational screen time per day. By automating these limits, Amelia ensures that each child has a consistent experience, allowing her to focus on quality time together rather than constantly monitoring device use.

Creating an Accountability System

In addition to using technology to manage device use, establishing an accountability system helps children take ownership of their screen time habits. A simple way to do this is by creating a family checklist or a reward chart where children can track their adherence to screen time rules. This system encourages children to stay mindful of their digital habits, rewarding them for following guidelines and motivating them to be responsible users.

For younger children, a reward chart with stickers or small rewards can make the experience engaging. Older children and teens may appreciate a points system, where points can be exchanged for privileges like extra screen time on weekends or choosing a family activity. This approach not only incentivises adherence to the media plan but also teaches children the importance of managing their screen time responsibly.

Consider Carlos and his children, who use a simple points system to track screen time adherence. Each child receives a point for every day they stay within their designated screen time, and points can be traded for a special family movie night or an extra 30 minutes of screen time on the weekend. This system has given Carlos's children a sense of control and responsibility over their digital habits, helping them internalise the importance of balance.

Reinforcing Guidelines Through Positive Communication

Positive communication plays a crucial role in strengthening screen time guidelines. Instead of focusing on what children can't do with their devices, parents can highlight the benefits of balanced device use and the joys of offline activities. By framing screen time rules as part of a healthy lifestyle, parents can create a positive attitude toward screen time boundaries, making children more willing to follow them.

For instance, rather than saying, "You're not allowed to use your device now," a parent could say, "Let's put away our devices for a bit and go outside for some fresh air." This reframing helps children see screen time limits as part of a balanced life rather than as restrictive rules. Positive reinforcement, such as praise or acknowledgment for respecting screen time limits, further motivates children to stay engaged with the family media plan.

Reflecting on the Benefits of the Family Media Plan

As families continue to implement their media plan, it's valuable to periodically reflect on the positive changes they notice. Families might find that with a structured approach to screen time, they experience more family bonding, improved communication, and greater involvement in offline activities. Regularly recognising these benefits helps strengthen the importance of the plan and encourages everyone to continue following the guidelines.

Ellie, a mother of two, uses positive language to encourage device-free moments at home. When her children put down their tablets during dinner, she thanks them and shares how much she values their company without screens. Her appreciation fosters pride and motivates her children to follow the family's screen time rules willingly.

MASTERING PARENTAL CONTROLS SETTINGS

The internet offers children a world of information, entertainment, and educational opportunities, but it also contains material that may not be suitable for their age. Parental controls and safety settings allow parents to model the online experience to be safer and more age appropriate. By using these tools thoughtfully, parents can enable their children to explore the digital world without exposing them to content they're not ready for. Parental controls provide a valuable layer of security, helping to manage what children can see and do online, as well as how long they engage with digital media.

Why Parental Controls Are a Valuable Tool

Parental controls aren't meant to limit a child's curiosity or restrict their learning; rather, they create a secure environment where children can safely develop their understanding of the online world. These tools allow parents to customise access on individual devices, filtering out unsuitable content and limiting screen time in a way that promotes a balanced digital life. Using parental controls helps reassure both parents and children, establishing boundaries that support healthy habits and safe exploration.

Emma, a mother of an 8-year-old named Liam, uses parental controls on his tablet to manage his viewing options. She has enabled a restricted profile through YouTube Kids, which blocks inappropriate content while allowing Liam to enjoy age-appropriate videos. By explaining these settings to him, Emma has helped Liam understand that his tablet is set up to show videos that are suitable for his age. This open approach has reassured Liam, and he feels comfortable exploring his tablet, knowing it's safe.

Types of Parental Controls and Their Benefits

Parental controls come in various forms and can be modified to fit a family's unique needs. Many devices, apps, and services have built-in parental controls, offering options to filter content, restrict downloads, and limit in-app purchases. Some of the most common parental control features include:

1. Content Filtering: Filters block websites and media that contain explicit or age-inappropriate content, allowing children to access only the resources that fit their age group.

2. Screen Time Limits: Many devices offer customisable time limits, automatically restricting access after a set period to prevent excessive screen use. This feature is especially helpful for managing screen time without constant reminders.

3. Purchase Controls: These settings restrict purchases within apps, avoiding unintended expenses and providing parents with more control over what children download or buy.

Implementing Parental Controls Across Multiple Devices

In households with multiple devices, it's essential to implement parental controls across each one that a child may use. Many families set up consistent controls on smartphones, tablets, and laptops, ensuring uniform protection across all platforms. By synchronising settings, parents can create a cohesive safety net, so that no matter which device their child uses, it's equipped with the same safety features.

Carlos, father of two children aged 10 and 14, has set up device controls tailored to each child's age. He installed a family safety app that tracks screen time and enforces content restrictions across all devices. This approach simplifies monitoring, keeping Carlos informed without being overly invasive. By using these tools consistently, Carlos has created a safe and predictable digital environment for his children.

Setting Up Parental Controls on Popular Platforms and Devices

Each digital platform and device come with unique parental control options. Understanding these settings can help parents customise a child's online experience in a way that fits their age, needs, and maturity level. Here, we'll explore some of the most widely used platforms and provide a step-by-step approach to configuring parental controls.

A parent setting up parental controls on a tablet

1. Smartphones and Tablets: iOS and Android

Both iOS and Android devices offer built-in parental controls to help manage content and limit screen time.

- For iOS (Apple Devices):
    - Navigate to Settings > Screen Time and select the child's device.
    - From here, parents can set daily screen time limits, block inappropriate content, and restrict specific apps or features.
    - Downtime can also be scheduled, automatically blocking access to most apps during specified hours, such as bedtime.
- For Android Devices:
    - Go to Settings > Digital Wellbeing & Parental Controls.
    - Set up a Family Link account, which allows parents to monitor and control app usage, content, and screen time from their own device.
    - With Family Link, parents can also set bedtime routines that automatically lock the child's device at designated times.

Emma set up Screen Time on her son Liam's iPad to manage app usage and limit video time. She restricted YouTube Kids to one hour daily, ensuring balanced screen time. This gives Emma peace of mind without needing constant monitoring.

2. Streaming Services: YouTube Kids and Netflix

Streaming platforms often provide parental control features to restrict inappropriate content, ensuring children only have access to age-appropriate media.

- YouTube Kids:
    - YouTube Kids is a safer alternative to the main YouTube app, offering pre-filtered content for children.
    - Parents can select "Approved Content Only" mode, which restricts access to handpicked videos and channels.

- Additionally, YouTube Kids has a Timer feature that limits session duration, prompting children to take breaks.
- Netflix:
    - Parents can create a "Kids Profile" on Netflix, which automatically filters content based on age ratings.
    - By going to Account Settings > Parental Controls, parents can add PIN protection to restrict certain content and adjust viewing limits based on age.

Carlos uses both YouTube Kids and Netflix to provide safe viewing options for his 10-year-old daughter. He has configured her YouTube Kids profile to access only approved content and set a timer that locks the app after 45 minutes. On Netflix, her Kids Profile restricts content to G-rated and PG-rated shows. This setup allows Carlos to feel confident about his daughter's streaming choices, knowing they align with their family's viewing guidelines.

3. Gaming Consoles and Online Games

Video game consoles, like PlayStation, Xbox, and Nintendo Switch, offer parental controls that restrict online interactions and limit game time.

- PlayStation (PS5):
    - Under Settings > Family and Parental Controls, parents can set time limits for gaming, manage spending, and restrict online multiplayer interactions.
    - Additionally, they can set content restrictions, preventing access to games with mature ratings.
- Xbox:
    - In Settings > Family Settings, Xbox allows parents to set screen time limits, restrict games by age rating, and manage in-game communication.
    - With the Xbox Family App, parents can monitor activity and adjust settings remotely.
- Nintendo Switch:
    - The Nintendo Switch Parental Controls app offers screen time tracking, playtime limits, and content restrictions.

o Parents can also restrict access to online multiplayer games, ensuring younger children don't interact with strangers in games.

Monica set up the Nintendo Switch Parental Controls app for her son Jake to limit his gaming to one hour on school nights and restrict online communication to pre-approved friends. This allows Jake to enjoy gaming while giving Monica peace of mind.

A parent configuring settings on YouTube Kids and a gaming console

Regularly Reviewing and Updating Settings

It's important for parents to regularly review and adjust parental control settings as children grow and their online needs change. Revisiting these settings helps ensure they remain relevant and effective, allowing parents to gradually introduce more flexibility as children demonstrate responsible behaviour.

Using Parental Controls as Part of a Broader Digital Responsibility Strategy

While parental controls provide a secure framework, they're only one aspect of nurturing responsible digital behaviour in children. By combining these controls with open discussions and guidance, parents can help children develop the skills they need to navigate the digital world responsibly. This approach encourages children to see parental controls as a form of support rather than restriction, helping them gradually learn to make safe, independent choices online.

1. Teaching Children About Privacy and Security

Parental controls are an effective way to protect privacy, but it's essential for children to understand why privacy matters. Teaching them about online security, including how to keep personal information safe, allows them to make wise decisions when they start using the internet independently. Parents can explain the importance of safeguarding personal details, such as their real name, address, school name, and photos, especially when interacting online.

Laura, mother of 13-year-old Clara, regularly discusses online privacy with her. When Clara started using social media, Laura explained the importance of keeping details like location and school private. She emphasised that online privacy settings are there to protect her from sharing too much with strangers. By discussing the purpose of these privacy controls, Laura helped Clara understand that these settings protect her from unwanted attention, encouraging her to take charge of her own privacy.

2. Developing Digital Etiquette *and Respect for Boundaries*

In addition to online safety, it's crucial for children to learn respectful online behaviour. Parental controls can limit interactions on certain platforms, but guiding children on how to behave in online spaces builds their confidence in managing interactions themselves. By teaching digital etiquette, parents can help children understand how to communicate respectfully, recognise cyberbullying, and avoid oversharing.

Carlos, a father of two, took the opportunity to talk to his 10-year-old son about digital etiquette when he began playing online games. They discussed what constitutes respectful language, the importance of respecting others' boundaries, and how to react if he encountered rude or hurtful comments. By setting these expectations early, Carlos helped his son develop a sense of responsibility for his online interactions, reducing the need for stringent controls as he matures.

3. Encouraging Self-Monitoring and Mindful Use of Technology

Parental controls can automatically manage screen time, but developing self-monitoring skills helps children recognise their own limits and make responsible choices. Encouraging children to be mindful of how much time they spend online, what activities they engage in, and how it makes them feel promotes a sense of ownership over their digital habits. Parents can start by having conversations about how different types of content make their children feel, emphasising the benefits of balancing screen time with other activities.

For instance, John noticed that his teenage daughter, Anna, sometimes felt drained after long social media sessions. He encouraged her to start noticing when she felt this way and suggested she take short breaks whenever she began to feel tired. Over time, Anna learned to recognise her limits and now uses a timer to remind herself to take breaks. John's approach helped Anna develop self-awareness and responsibility in her digital habits, encouraging her to use technology mindfully.

4. Strengthening the Purpose of Parental Controls with Positive Communication

Openly discussing the purpose of parental controls and emphasising their role in promoting a safe environment reinforces trust between parents and children. When children understand that these controls are there to protect them, rather than limit their freedom, they are more likely to cooperate and respect the boundaries. Parents can remind their children that as they grow and demonstrate responsible behaviour, they will gain more independence with online activities.

Peter explains the purpose of each control to her 8-year-old son, Liam, whenever he sets up a new restriction. Recently, when he added a new screen time limit on his tablet, Peter sat down with Liam and explained that it was there to help him enjoy his other activities too. By framing these boundaries as part of a balanced lifestyle, Peter reinforced the positive role of parental controls, helping Liam view them as helpful tools rather than restrictions

Exploring Additional Tools and Resources for Digital Safety

In addition to built-in parental controls, a variety of tools and resources are available to support families in fostering digital safety. These resources complement parental controls by providing information, filtering services, and monitoring tools that enhance the security of online experiences. By integrating these tools into the family's digital routine, parents can create a more comprehensive safety network that adapts as their children's online habits evolve.

1. *Family Safety Apps*

Family safety apps, such as Qustodio, Bark, and Net Nanny, offer extensive options beyond standard parental controls. These apps allow parents to monitor screen time, track location, filter content, and receive alerts for potential issues, such as cyberbullying or suspicious interactions. By installing a family safety app, parents can gain insights into their children's online behaviour, giving them a clearer picture of how they spend time on devices and what types of content they interact with.

Carlos, who has two children with different online interests, found a family safety app particularly helpful for managing each child's needs individually. Through the app, he sets specific content filters and time limits for his younger child while allowing more flexibility for his teenage daughter. This app has allowed Carlos to address each child's unique habits and concerns, providing tailored support for both.

2. *Educational Websites and Digital Literacy Programs*

Teaching children about online safety can go beyond setting rules; it can also involve educating them on digital literacy. Websites like Common Sense Media, Google's Be Internet Awesome, and Cyber

Civics provide age-appropriate resources that help children understand digital safety, privacy, and respectful online behaviour. These platforms provide interactive games, videos, and lessons that engage children in learning essential skills for exploring the digital world.

For instance, Laura uses Be Internet Awesome to strengthen digital safety skills with her 11-year-old son, Alex. They explore interactive activities together, learning about password safety, identifying online scams, and understanding digital footprints. These activities have become part of their weekly routine, helping Alex adopt safety concepts through a fun, hands-on approach. By integrating these lessons, Laura has enabled Alex to approach the internet with awareness and caution.

3. Browser Extensions and Search Engine Filters

Browser extensions and search engine filters provide an extra layer of security for children who explore the internet for schoolwork or entertainment. Tools like SafeSearch for Google, Kidslox, and BlockSite help filter inappropriate content, block pop-ups, and prevent access to distracting or unsafe sites. These settings can be enabled on family devices, ensuring children have a secure browsing environment when using search engines or accessing websites independently.

Emma, a mother of an 8-year-old, has set up Google SafeSearch on all family devices. This feature automatically filters explicit content from search results, allowing her son to research topics for school projects safely. Additionally, Emma uses a browser extension that blocks ad pop-ups, reducing the chance of her son accidentally clicking on misleading ads or malicious links. These simple measures have given Emma confidence that her son's browsing experience remains secure.

4. Device-Specific Controls and Customisation

Many tech companies now offer device-specific parental controls and customisation options, such as the Amazon Fire Kids Edition and Apple's Family Sharing. These devices often come with pre-configured safety features, such as content limits, app restrictions, and time controls that make it easier to manage children's activities without needing additional software. Such devices provide parents with peace of mind, knowing they're designed to prioritise children's safety from the outset.

Monica recently purchased an Amazon Fire Kids Edition tablet for her daughter, Zoe, who is 7. The tablet comes with a child-friendly interface, customisable time limits, and age-appropriate content filters that align with their family's media plan. This setup has allowed Zoe to explore independently, while Monica feels secure knowing the device is designed for safe usage. The built-in controls provide a worry-free experience, allowing Zoe to enjoy her tablet without frequent adjustments.

Regularly Reviewing and Updating Tools

As new tools and features become available, parents can review and update their digital safety strategies. Revisiting family settings and trying out different resources regularly ensures the approach stays relevant, especially as children mature and their digital needs evolve. By staying informed on the latest safety tools, parents can adapt to changing online trends, keeping their family's digital environment secure and aligned with their values.

Maintaining an Open Dialogue About Digital Safety

Parental controls and safety tools can protect children from many online risks, but regular conversations about digital safety are crucial to help them navigate the digital world confidently and responsibly. By making discussions about online experiences a part of daily life, parents create an environment where children feel comfortable sharing questions or concerns as they arise. This ongoing dialogue not only strengthens family bonds but also prepares children to make informed decisions about their digital habits as they grow.

1. Checking In on a Regular Basis

A consistent approach to digital check-ins allows children to share new experiences, voice any discomfort, and receive guidance on handling complex situations online. These conversations can be short and relaxed, such as a casual discussion during dinner or on the drive home from school. By showing genuine interest in their children's online lives, parents build a foundation of trust that encourages openness and honesty.

Take the example of John, who makes a habit of asking his teenage daughter about her day online. He asks questions like, "Did you see anything interesting online today?" or "Are there any new games your friends are playing?" This routine has allowed his daughter to share freely, including moments when she encounters content or interactions that make her uncomfortable. John's consistent, open approach has strengthened their relationship and ensured that his daughter feels safe coming to him with her online experiences.

Parent using a family safety app or exploring a digital literacy program with a child

2. Making Adjustments as Children Grow

As children mature, their digital needs and interests change. Revisiting parental controls and online safety guidelines at regular intervals allows parents to adjust the level of support based on each child's age, maturity, and experience. When children demonstrate responsible behaviour, gradually relaxing certain restrictions shows them that their efforts to follow guidelines are valued. This balanced approach empowers children to gain independence while remaining mindful of family values.

Laura, a mother of a 14-year-old son, periodically reviews his device settings to ensure they fit his current needs. Recently, she adjusted his screen time limits, allowing an extra hour on weekends, given his positive attitude toward managing school and family commitments. Laura's willingness to adapt the rules has shown her son that responsible behaviour leads to increased trust and independence, reinforcing the family's shared commitment to digital safety.

3. Fostering Critical Thinking and Problem-Solving Skills

While parental controls provide immediate protection, developing critical thinking skills enables children to recognise unfamiliar or risky online situations independently. Teaching children to question the credibility of content, recognise online scams, and handle uncomfortable interactions equips them to make safer choices. Parents can model these skills by discussing real-life examples and asking questions that encourage children to think critically about what they see online.

Carlos, for instance, frequently discusses online safety scenarios with his 10-year-old daughter. They talk about "What if…" situations, such as "What if someone asks you for your personal information?" or "What would you do if you saw something that seemed too good to be true?" These conversations have helped Carlos's daughter learn to recognise potential online risks and develop a proactive approach to staying safe, even beyond the scope of parental controls.

4. Reinforcing the Value of Balance and Offline Activities

Encouraging children to embrace offline activities as part of their daily routine promotes a healthy relationship with technology. By setting aside time for non-digital pursuits—like sports, hobbies, or family activities—parents can show children that a balanced lifestyle enhances well-being. These moments away from screens strengthen the idea that technology is just one part of life, not the entirety.

Emma, a mother of two, has established a tradition of "offline Sundays" where the family puts away devices and engages in outdoor activities, games, or cooking together. Her children have come to appreciate these screen-free days, seeing them as a special time to connect with each other and recharge. By setting this example, Emma demonstrates the value of balance and helps her children view screen time as one aspect of a well-rounded lifestyle.

Reflecting on the Family's Digital Journey

Regularly reflecting on the benefits of these strategies, both as a family and individually, encourages everyone to stay committed to digital safety. Parents can celebrate milestones, like successfully following the family media plan or showing responsibility with a new app, acknowledging the progress each family member makes. These reflections boost the family's commitment to online safety and develop a positive outlook toward managing digital habits

MONITORING ONLINE ACTIVITY

With children increasingly interacting with the digital world, monitoring online activity has become a crucial element of digital safety. By regularly checking in on their children's online habits, parents can gain valuable insights into what interests them, where they might be exposed to potential risks, and how they spend their time online. Monitoring isn't about intruding on children's privacy; rather, it's a way to support their growth by creating a safe, balanced online experience. Through thoughtful observation and regular check-ins, parents can guide children toward responsible and mindful digital habits.

The Purpose of Monitoring

Monitoring online activity offers several benefits that extend beyond simply keeping children safe. It helps parents understand their children's evolving interests, which can change frequently as they explore new apps, games, and content. This understanding allows parents to stay engaged and connected, opening doors for conversations that strengthen family values and provide guidance on appropriate online behaviour. By approaching monitoring as a supportive tool, parents can create a trusting environment where children feel comfortable discussing their online experiences without fear of punishment.

Carlos, a father of two, uses a regular check of the family computer's browsing history to stay informed about his teenage son's interests. Recently, he noticed his son had been researching topics related to game design, sparking a conversation about his son's aspirations in technology. Through this routine, Carlos not only gained insight into his son's interests but also provided encouragement, supporting his growth in a constructive way. Carlos's approach to monitoring illustrates how thoughtful observation can strengthen family connections while keeping children safe

Balancing Privacy and Safety

Striking the right balance between monitoring and respecting a child's privacy can be challenging, particularly as children grow older and seek more independence. Setting clear expectations from the beginning is essential. When children understand that monitoring is a way for parents to keep them safe, not to invade their privacy, they're more likely to accept and respect this aspect of online safety. Parents can reassure children that as they show responsibility, they'll gain more freedom and privacy with their devices.

Laura, a mother of a 13-year-old daughter, emphasises this balance by openly discussing her monitoring practices with her daughter. She explains that while she occasionally checks her daughter's social media profiles, her goal isn't to pry but to ensure her safety. Laura's approach has promoted an open line of communication, where her daughter feels confident sharing her online interactions without the fear of being overly scrutinised. By reinforcing her intention to protect, Laura has cultivated a relationship of trust that supports her daughter's independence.

Choosing the Right Level of Monitoring

The level of monitoring should be age-appropriate, adjusting as children demonstrate responsibility and understanding of online safety. Younger children may need closer observation and guidance, while older children and teenagers might benefit from occasional check-ins. Setting an initial level of monitoring and then adjusting it over time allows parents to gradually build trust and give children more freedom as they mature. This flexible approach reinforces that online safety is a shared responsibility between parent and child.

Emma, who has both a young child and a teenager, tailors her monitoring practices to each child's age. For her younger child, she closely reviews the apps and games he accesses, ensuring they're appropriate. With her teenage daughter, Emma maintains occasional check-ins, letting her know that she's available if anything concerning arises. This balance has helped her children understand that monitoring varies by age and maturity, making them feel supported rather than restricted.

*P*arent reviewing browsing history with a child or discussing online interests

Practical Methods for Monitoring

Monitoring doesn't have to be intrusive or complex. There are several practical ways for parents to stay informed about their children's online behaviour while respecting their privacy. By using subtle, consistent methods, parents can keep an eye on activity patterns, identify potential risks, and provide support without making children feel like they're under constant surveillance.

1. Reviewing Browsing History and App Usage

Checking a child's browsing history or app usage can give parents a snapshot of their interests and habits. Browsing history shows the types of websites children visit, while app usage provides insight into how they spend their time online. Setting a regular schedule to review this activity helps parents stay informed and detect any potentially harmful trends or interests.

Carlos, a father who regularly reviews his 10-year-old son's browsing history, uses this approach to keep their online interactions safe. One day, he noticed that his son had searched for information on downloading free games from untrustworthy websites. This observation sparked a conversation about the risks of downloading from unfamiliar sources, such as exposure to malware and viruses. Carlos's subtle monitoring allowed him to catch a potential risk and guide his son without being overly intrusive.

2. Using Parental Control Apps for Transparency

Parental control apps can provide monitoring support by tracking device usage, app downloads, and screen time in a way that's less invasive. These apps allow parents to set screen time limits and receive usage reports, helping them stay informed about digital habits without the need for constant check-ins. Many parental control apps also offer age-appropriate filters, ensuring that children can only access suitable content.

Monica, a mother of two, uses a parental control app to monitor her children's screen time and app downloads. She receives weekly usage reports, allowing her to see how much time her children spend on different activities. Recently, the app alerted her that her 12-year-old son had downloaded a social media app without permission. This prompted a discussion about why they limit certain apps and the importance of transparency. By using a control app, Monica maintains a gentle presence in her children's online world, ensuring she stays aware of any changes in their habits.

3. Establishing Open Communication About Monitoring

Children are more likely to accept monitoring when they understand its purpose and limitations. By establishing clear guidelines around how and why monitoring is used, parents help children see it as a part of online safety rather than a lack of trust. Reinforcing that monitoring will become less frequent as children show responsibility allows them to see it as a supportive measure, not a restriction.

Emma openly discusses her monitoring practices with her teenage daughter, letting her know which apps and platforms she checks and why. By being transparent, Emma has built trust, and her daughter understands that as she continues to demonstrate responsible behaviour, Emma's checks will gradually decrease. This communication has made monitoring feel less intrusive and more like a partnership focused on safety.

4. Observing Social Media and Online Interactions Carefully

For older children and teens, social media is often a major part of their online life. Monitoring social media interactions can help parents detect any signs of cyberbullying, exposure to inappropriate content, or unsafe connections. However, it's important to approach this aspect carefully, as teens may be sensitive about their social circles. Periodically reviewing social media activity or checking privacy settings can be a subtle way to ensure safety.

John, whose daughter recently joined Instagram, set up an initial agreement to review her profile and privacy settings together once a month. They discuss who she follows, her privacy settings, and any messages that might be questionable. This approach keeps John informed while allowing his daughter a sense of privacy and autonomy. By focusing on her safety rather than strict oversight, John has been able to support her online presence responsibly.

Keeping Monitoring Consistent and Positive

Consistency is key to effective monitoring. When parents are consistent with check-ins or app usage reports, children become accustomed to these routines, reducing feelings of intrusion. Maintaining a positive tone and framing monitoring as a safety tool reinforces a child's understanding of its purpose, helping them develop digital habits that promote independence and responsibility.

A p*arent and child reviewing app usage and discussing social media privacy settings*

Age-Appropriate Monitoring Strategies

Monitoring strategies are most effective when adapted to a child's age and developmental stage. As children grow, they develop new interests and may encounter different online challenges. By adjusting monitoring practices to align with each stage of development, parents can provide the right level of guidance, gradually enabling children to make responsible choices independently.

1. Early Childhood (Ages 5-8): Close Supervision and Simple Controls

For younger children who are new to using digital devices, close supervision is essential. At this age, children are often curious and may not yet recognise potential online risks. Monitoring practices for this age group should focus on actively guiding children through apps and games, ensuring they only access age-appropriate content, and setting time limits to prevent excessive use.

Emma, a mother of a 6-year-old, limits her son's device use to specific educational apps. She uses a child-friendly tablet with pre-installed apps and content filters, which allows her to closely monitor his activity. Whenever he finishes using the device, Emma checks his activity and reinforces safety concepts by discussing what he enjoyed about the app. Her approach allows her son to explore technology in a safe and controlled way, ensuring that his early online experiences are positive.

2. Middle Childhood (Ages 9-12): Increasing Independence with Supervision

In middle childhood, children begin to seek more independence and may show interest in exploring online games, videos, and simple social features. Monitoring practices should still involve direct oversight, but parents can start teaching children basic safety practices, such as avoiding strangers and recognising unsuitable content. Parental control apps that offer screen time limits and content filters can help support this transition, gradually giving children more freedom within established boundaries.

Carlos, who has a 10-year-old daughter, uses a parental control app to set time limits and filter content on her tablet. He also discusses her activity with her each week, asking questions like, "What games are you enjoying?" and "Did you find anything new online that was interesting?" These conversations allow Carlos to keep an eye on her interests, guiding her toward safe choices without restricting her independence.

3. Early Teens (Ages 13-15): Guidance and Limited Monitoring

During early adolescence, teens begin to engage with more complex content, including social media, multiplayer games, and independent research for school. At this stage, monitoring should focus on supporting teens' growing independence by setting clear boundaries and guiding responsible choices. While direct oversight may be reduced, parents can still perform periodic checks of browsing history, social media profiles, and app usage to ensure safety.

Laura, whose son is 14, has adopted a "trust and verify" approach. She provides guidance on privacy settings and online etiquette, allowing her son to manage his accounts with minimal intervention. They have an agreement to review his social media privacy settings monthly, and he knows that Laura will occasionally check his browsing history. By being open about her expectations, Laura has built a trusting relationship that supports her son's independence while ensuring he understands the importance of online safety.

4. Older Teens (Ages 16+): Minimal Monitoring and Open Communication

Older teens generally value privacy and independence, and many have developed a sense of responsibility with online behaviour. For this age group, minimal monitoring is often sufficient, with a focus on open communication. Parents can emphasise the importance of digital responsibility, providing guidance as needed while allowing teens to navigate online spaces independently.

Adapting Monitoring as Children Grow

As children move through different stages, parents can adjust monitoring practices to gradually provide more independence, fostering trust and respect. Revisiting and adapting monitoring strategies based on each child's maturity level ensures that they receive the guidance they need while gaining the skills to make safe, responsible choices.

Age-appropriate monitoring methods, from close supervision to independent guidance.

Addressing Challenges and Handling Resistance to Monitoring

As children grow, they may feel that monitoring invades their privacy, especially as they seek more independence online. This pushback reflects their desire for trust and respect. Parents can address this by fostering open, respectful conversations, helping children see monitoring as a supportive measure, not a restriction. This approach reduces resistance and strengthens the parent-child relationship, encouraging children to view monitoring as part of their shared commitment to digital safety.

1. Emphasising Trust and Safety

One effective way to reduce resistance is by emphasising that monitoring is based on trust, not control. Parents can explain that as children demonstrate responsible behaviour online, monitoring will gradually decrease, allowing them more freedom and independence. By framing monitoring as a tool that protects rather than restricts, parents help children feel valued and respected.

Carlos, for instance, noticed that his 13-year-old son had started to resent regular checks of his browsing history. To address this, Carlos had a open conversation with his son, explaining that he valued his son's growing independence and that these checks were simply a way to ensure his safety as he explored new online spaces. Carlos assured him that as he continued to make responsible choices, the checks would become less frequent. This transparency reassured his son, who now views the checks as part of a gradual process toward increased trust and freedom.

2. Engaging Children in Setting Boundaries

Involving children in discussions about digital boundaries can help reduce resistance, as it gives them a voice in shaping the family's online safety practices. By working together to establish guidelines, parents can better align monitoring practices with children's comfort levels, making them feel like active participants rather than passive recipients of rules. This collaboration can also lead to creative solutions that meet both parents' and children's needs.

For example, Laura's daughter, a 15-year-old, felt uncomfortable with the idea of her mother checking her social media messages. To find a compromise, Laura suggested they review her social media privacy settings together instead, focusing on managing friend requests and reporting inappropriate content. By respecting her daughter's boundaries, Laura fostered a sense of partnership and trust, making her daughter more open to following the agreed-upon guidelines.

3. Using Positive Reinforcement for Cooperation

Positive reinforcement is a valuable tool in managing resistance to monitoring. By recognising and rewarding responsible behaviour, parents can encourage children to follow digital safety guidelines willingly. Positive feedback strengthens good habits and encourages children to make smart choices online, promoting a more cooperative attitude toward supervision.

Emma, a mother of an 11-year-old, has implemented a simple reward system where her son earns privileges, like extra screen time on weekends, for following their family's screen time and safety guidelines. This approach has helped her son view monitoring in a positive way, associating it with encouragement rather than restriction. Emma's positive reinforcement has made monitoring feel like a supportive part of their routine, rather than a control measure.

4. Reassuring Older Children About Privacy

Privacy is essential for teenagers as they develop their independence. Parents can show respect for this need by gradually reducing direct oversight as children demonstrate responsible digital behaviour. Regular conversations that acknowledge their need for privacy help teens feel respected and less defensive about monitoring. By shifting from hands-on monitoring to open communication, parents can show teens that they're trusted to make safe decisions.

John, whose daughter is 17, has transitioned from regular monitoring to occasional discussions about online safety. He periodically checks in with her about any concerns or challenges she's facing online, allowing her to bring up topics on her own terms. This approach has preserved her privacy while keeping John engaged in her digital life, maintaining a balance that respects her independence while supporting her safety.

Building a Lasting Foundation of Trust

When children view monitoring as part of a broader strategy for digital safety, they're more likely to accept it as a positive, supportive measure. By approaching monitoring with respect for teens' privacy, involving them in setting boundaries, and rewarding responsible behaviour, parents can build a lasting foundation of trust that goes beyond childhood.

The Long-Term Benefits of Monitoring as a Tool for Building Digital Responsibility

Monitoring isn't only a means of ensuring immediate safety; it's also an investment in building digital responsibility that will benefit children for years to come. When used carefully, monitoring teaches children essential skills, such as managing their time, making responsible choices, and handling online challenges. By guiding children through their digital experiences with a balanced approach, parents help them develop the skills to handle the online world independently as they grow older.

A parent and teen discussing online privacy and collaboratively setting digital boundaries

1. Developing Time Management and Self-Regulation

One of the most valuable lessons that monitoring instils is time management. Screen time limits and app usage reports help children become more aware of how much time they spend online, encouraging a balanced approach to digital activities. By understanding their usage patterns, children learn to prioritise schoolwork, hobbies, and family time, encouraging healthy habits that extend into adulthood.

Carlos has seen this growth firsthand with his 14-year-old son, who now independently follows screen time guidelines without reminders. This shift has been a gradual process, starting with parental controls that restricted screen time and transitioning to self-regulation as his son showed responsibility. This journey taught Carlos's son how to balance his time effectively, a skill that has benefited his overall routine and well-being.

2. Strengthening Critical Thinking and Digital Literacy

As children face various forms of content online, monitoring can serve as a basis for developing critical thinking skills. Parents can use monitoring as a springboard for conversations about credible information, online risks, and personal responsibility. Teaching children to question and assess the content they encounter prepares them for the challenges of digital media, helping them tell fact from fiction and avoid scams.

Laura, a mother of two, has used monitoring to strengthen her children's critical thinking skills. Whenever she notices her kids watching or reading something questionable, she engages them in a discussion, asking questions like, "What makes this source reliable?" or "Does this sound too good to be true?" These conversations have prepared her children to handle digital content independently, giving them a solid foundation in digital literacy that will benefit them as they grow.

3. Building Trust and Communication Skills

Consistent monitoring, when approached with openness, builds trust and strengthens parent-child communication. By keeping the lines of communication open, parents encourage children to discuss their online experiences, building transparency and mutual respect. These skills are invaluable, not only for digital safety but also for building trust and honesty in other areas of life.

Emma, whose son is in his early teens, has found that the trust they built around monitoring extends to other aspects of their relationship. By consistently discussing online safety, she has created a safe space where her son feels comfortable sharing his challenges and asking for guidance. This trust has deepened their bond and has made Emma's son more open to discussing sensitive topics, reinforcing the value of communication.

4. Preparing for Independent Digital Citizenship

Monitoring prepares children for independent digital citizenship. As they grow, children will encounter new platforms, content, and interactions, often outside their parents' oversight. Through gradual exposure, guidance, and support, monitoring helps children develop a sense of accountability for their actions online, ensuring they carry family values and responsible habits into adulthood.

John's approach with his teenage daughter reflects this goal of independent digital citizenship. By transitioning from strict monitoring to open dialogue, John has instilled in his daughter a sense of responsibility and respect for her online choices. Now, as she navigates the online world independently, she carries with her the principles and skills cultivated through years of supportive guidance.

Celebrating Progress and Encouraging Lifelong Learning

As children become more skilled at managing their digital lives, it's beneficial to celebrate their progress. Acknowledging milestones, such as managing screen time independently or practicing safe online interactions, reinforces positive habits and builds confidence. Encouraging children to continue learning about digital safety also reminds them that responsible digital behaviour is a lifelong journey, one that evolves as technology and their needs change.

TEACHING DIGITAL CITIZENSHIP

Understanding Digital Citizenship and Its Importance

Digital citizenship involves the values, behaviours, and practices that guide responsible and respectful participation in online communities. As children grow and explore a variety of digital platforms—like social media, educational sites, or gaming communities—they need the skills to engage in these spaces with respect, empathy, and awareness. Teaching digital citizenship involves more than rules; it's about teaching values that encourage children to treat others kindly, recognise online boundaries, and consider the impact of their actions on others.

Digital citizenship serves as a foundation for safe and positive online experiences. By learning to respect others, protect their privacy, and avoid harmful behaviours like cyberbullying, children build a sense of responsibility that extends beyond the screen. They become mindful, informed users who can positively contribute to digital spaces while keeping themselves safe from risks. Building these skills early prepares children to make wise choices and commit to responsible online behaviour for life.

Emma, a mother of two, introduced digital citizenship to her children when they began using online games and social media. By stressing respect for others and explaining the consequences of hurtful language, Emma has helped her children see online spaces as extensions of real life, where kindness and empathy are just as important. Through her guidance, Emma has set clear expectations for respectful online behaviour, providing her children with a framework to navigate digital communities responsibly.

1. Encouraging Empathy and Respect in Online Interactions

One of the core principles of digital citizenship is empathy. Children who understand empathy recognise that their actions and words can affect others, even in virtual settings. Teaching children to consider others' feelings, avoid negative comments, and support peers encourages them to contribute positively to online communities. Parents can encourage empathy by discussing real-life scenarios or by sharing stories about respectful online behaviour.

Consider Carlos, who noticed that his son, while playing online games, sometimes encountered players who used harsh language or made rude comments. Carlos took this opportunity to talk to his son about empathy, explaining that even though it's an online space, the people on the other side are real and can be affected by hurtful words. Together, they discussed how to respond positively and how to avoid interactions that didn't feel respectful. By framing online behaviour as a reflection of real-life values, Carlos reinforced the importance of empathy in his son's digital life.

2. Teaching Responsible Sharing and Privacy Awareness

Teaching children about responsible sharing is an essential part of digital citizenship. Children should understand that once information is shared online, it can be difficult to take back. Parents can encourage children to think carefully about what they post, reminding them that personal details, such as location, school, or private photos, should be kept off public platforms. By emphasising the importance of privacy, parents help children avoid sharing information that could compromise their safety.

Laura, a mother of a teenage daughter, used an example from the news about privacy risks to start a conversation with her daughter. She explained why it's important to think twice before sharing personal information and why certain details should only be shared with close friends or family. Laura's approach helped her daughter understand that while sharing online can be fun, it's essential to prioritise safety. This understanding has made her daughter more cautious about what she posts, knowing that online privacy is something to be safeguarded.

Parent and child discussing online behaviour, with examples of empathy and privacy

Identifying and Addressing Cyberbullying

Cyberbullying, or bullying that occurs online, is a significant concern for children and teens who partake in digital communities. Unlike traditional bullying, cyberbullying can happen anytime and in any digital space, making it widespread and harder for children to escape. Teaching children to recognise the signs of cyberbullying—whether directed at them or others—is a key part of digital citizenship. By learning to manage negative online behaviour, children can protect themselves, support others, and help create a safer online environment.

Parents can begin by discussing what cyberbullying includes, such as hurtful messages, exclusion, spreading rumours, and sharing embarrassing images or personal information without consent. Once children understand these behaviours, they're better prepared to recognise them and take action if they encounter or witness cyberbullying. Encouraging children to report inappropriate behaviour and providing tools to block or mute harmful users help them take control of their digital interactions.

Laura, whose daughter recently started using social media, introduced her to the concept of cyberbullying through real-life examples and news stories. She explained that if her daughter ever felt uncomfortable or saw someone being treated unfairly online, she should tell her parents, report the behaviour, or use the platform's blocking features. Laura's approach has made her daughter more confident in recognising inappropriate behaviour, helping her feel empowered to take action if she ever encounters cyberbullying.

1. Teaching Children to Report and Block Harmful Behaviour

Reporting and blocking tools are available on most social media platforms, gaming networks, and messaging apps. Teaching children how to use these features allows them to manage their interactions and protect themselves from harmful behaviour. Encouraging children to report inappropriate behaviour—whether they experience it directly or see it happen to someone else—contributes to creating a safer, more respectful online community.

Carlos recently taught his son how to block a user who was being rude during an online game. They went through the process together, with Carlos explaining that blocking someone is a form of self-protection, allowing his son to focus on positive interactions. Additionally, Carlos emphasised that reporting helps the platform identify and address harmful users, making it safer for everyone. This experience helped Carlos's son feel that he had control over his online environment, and he now understands that reporting inappropriate behaviour contributes to a healthier digital space.

2. Encouraging Children to Be an Ally

Digital citizenship involves not only protecting oneself but also supporting others. Children who understand empathy and kindness in online spaces are more likely to intervene when they witness cyberbullying. By teaching children how to be an ally—whether by offering support to a friend or reporting harmful behaviour on behalf of someone else—parents encourage a culture of respect and mutual protection. Being an ally also helps children understand that they can make a positive impact, strengthening their role as responsible members of digital communities.

Emma, whose son is 11, recently had a conversation with him about standing up for friends online. She explained that if he ever sees a friend being treated poorly, he can help by offering support, reporting the behaviour, or simply being there to listen. Emma's guidance has helped her son feel confident about supporting friends, and he now knows that he has the tools to make a difference in both his online and offline relationships. By encouraging this supportive mindset, Emma has encouraged her son to be proactive in creating positive digital spaces.

3. Reinforcing the Value of Kindness and Respect

In addition to reporting and blocking, teaching children to respond to harmful behaviour with kindness helps create a positive digital environment. While not every situation requires direct action, demonstrating kindness and respect—even when others don't—provides a powerful approach to handling online spaces. Parents can remind children that they have the ability to influence the tone of their interactions, encouraging respectful communication that reflects family values.

John, who has a teenage daughter, often talks to her about the impact of her words and actions, both online and in person. When his daughter encountered a rude comment on one of her posts, John encouraged her to respond calmly, if at all, and to consider whether a response was even necessary. This approach has helped John's daughter realise that she doesn't need to engage with negativity and that her actions can set an example of kindness for others.

A parent guiding a child through reporting or blocking features on a social media app

Responsible Information Sharing and Verifying Online Sources

In an age of vast information, teaching children to recognise credible sources and share information responsibly is an essential aspect of digital citizenship. With easy access to articles, videos, and social media posts, children may encounter misinformation or content that is exaggerated or unreliable. Teaching children to approach online content with critical thinking equips them to make informed decisions, avoid spreading false information, and understand the impact of what they share. One effective way to begin is by explaining that not everything on the internet is true or accurate. Encourage children to look for clues that indicate credibility, such as author credentials, the website's reputation, and evidence supporting the content. Helping children identify reputable sources, like educational websites, official news outlets, and peer-reviewed research, gives them a strong foundation for responsible information consumption.

1. Teaching Critical Thinking Skills for Information Evaluation

Critical thinking is a skill that helps children assess the validity of information before accepting or sharing it. By teaching children to ask questions like, "Who created this content?" "Why was it created?" and "Is there evidence to support it?" parents help them develop a habit of analysing information thoroughly. This skill can be strengthened through discussions about how to recognise bias, distinguish opinion from fact, and identify signs of credible journalism.

Carlos, a father of a 13-year-old daughter, encourages critical thinking by discussing current events together. They review articles from different sources and talk about any biases or perspectives presented. This approach has helped Carlos's daughter learn to identify opinion versus factual reporting and has made her more mindful about accepting information at face value. By fostering critical thinking, Carlos has equipped his daughter with the tools to navigate digital information thoughtfully.

2. Discussing the Impact of Sharing Misinformation

Children need to understand that sharing information online carries responsibility. Even a single share or repost can spread false information widely, affecting people's beliefs and decisions. Parents can discuss how misinformation can lead to confusion, fear, or even harm, encouraging children to think before they share. Reminding children that they should only share content that aligns with their values and meets credibility standards reinforces this sense of responsibility.

Laura recently spoke with her teenage son about the importance of sharing responsibly. When her son shared a humorous but questionable meme with his friends, Laura used the moment to discuss how even small actions contribute to the spread of ideas online. Together, they reviewed the meme's origin and found it was based on misinformation. This discussion helped her son realise the potential impact of his shares, making him more cautious about passing along content in the future.

3. Encouraging Fact-Checking Tools and Resources

A variety of fact-checking tools and resources are available to help children verify online information. Websites like Snopes, FactCheck.org, and educational extensions like Google's Fact Check Explorer can make it easier for children to assess the credibility of content they encounter. Teaching children how to use these resources enables them to verify information independently, reinforcing their critical thinking and digital literacy skills.

John recently introduced his daughter to a fact-checking website when she shared an article about a sensational news story. They used the tool to assess the article's credibility, discovering that parts of the story were unverified. This experience taught John's daughter the value of fact-checking and gave her a practical tool for future use. Now, she feels more confident in evaluating content independently, knowing she has the tools to verify information.

Reinforcing the Value of Reliable, Truthful Content

Teaching children to value credible information helps build a foundation for responsible digital behaviour focused on integrity and respect. Children who recognise the importance of reliable content become thoughtful digital citizens, positively contributing to online communities by sharing information that is truthful, respectful, and responsible.

John, who has a teenage daughter, often talks to her about the impact of her words and actions, both online and in person. When his daughter encountered a rude comment on one of her posts, John encouraged her to respond calmly, if at all, and to consider whether a response was even necessary. This approach has helped John's daughter understand that she doesn't need to engage with negative behaviour and that her actions can serve as an example of kindness for others.

A PRACTICAL GUIDE FOR PARENTS TO KEEP KIDS SAFE ONLINE

Parent and child using a fact-checking website together to verify information

Understanding Digital Footprints and Their Long-Term Impact

Every action taken online leaves a "digital footprint," a record of posts, comments, and interactions that remain accessible even long after they've been shared. Teaching children about digital footprints helps them understand that their online actions have lasting consequences, shaping how others perceive them and potentially influencing future opportunities. By approaching digital citizenship with this long-term perspective, children can make more thoughtful decisions, creating a positive, respectful online presence.

Digital footprints are created not only by public posts but also by private messages, photos, and online searches. Once something is shared, even with privacy settings, it can be difficult to completely erase.

Encouraging children to consider how their actions today might affect their reputation in the future fosters a sense of accountability and encourages them to be mindful of how they engage with others online.

Laura spoke with her teenage daughter about digital footprints after her daughter posted a photo with friends at a party. They discussed how sharing personal moments can be fun, but also how it's important to consider who might see the content and how it could be perceived. Laura reminded her daughter that even seemingly harmless posts can shape her digital identity, encouraging her to be mindful about sharing personal information and respecting her friends' privacy. This conversation helped Laura's daughter understand that her online choices contribute to her overall digital footprint.

1. *Thinking Before Posting*

One of the simplest yet most effective ways to manage a digital footprint is by thinking carefully before posting. Encouraging children to pause and reflect on questions like, "Is this something I'd want others to see in the future?" or "Would I feel comfortable sharing this with a larger audience?" helps them consider the long-term impact of their actions. Parents can model this habit by talking about the types of content they choose to share, showing that thoughtful sharing is a family value.

Carlos, for example, encourages his son to take a "pause and think" approach before sharing anything online. He explains that the internet is a public space, and even small comments or jokes can be taken out of context. By practicing this pause, Carlos's son has become more intentional about his online actions, developing a habit of considering the broader impact of what he posts or shares.

2. *Highlighting Privacy Settings and Secure Sharing Options*

Privacy settings on social media and messaging platforms can help children control who sees their content, but it's essential they understand that these settings don't guarantee complete privacy. Teaching children to use privacy settings effectively, while also cautioning them about potential sharing beyond these controls, helps them create a safer online environment. Parents can review privacy options with their children, ensuring they know how to manage friends lists, restrict visibility, and adjust privacy settings as needed.

Emma, whose 12-year-old daughter recently joined a social media platform, went through the privacy settings with her. Together, they set the profile to "friends only" and discussed the importance of not accepting friend requests from people she didn't know in real life. By involving her in the process, Emma emphasised that privacy is an active choice, helping her daughter feel more confident in managing her online presence responsibly.

3. Using the "Grandma Rule" for Positive Sharing

A helpful guideline for children is the "Grandma Rule"—if they wouldn't feel comfortable sharing something with their grandmother, they might want to think twice before posting it online. This light-hearted rule helps children visualise the potential audience for their content, reminding them that online actions are public and can reach a wider audience than expected. This rule encourages children to share positive, respectful content that reflects well on them.

John introduced his teenage daughter to the "Grandma Rule" when she first joined a social media platform. He explained that if she's unsure about a post, imagining how her grandmother would react can be a good indicator of its appropriateness. This advice resonated with his daughter, helping her adopt a more thoughtful approach to her posts and comments. The "Grandma Rule" has since become a family saying, reinforcing their shared value of respectful online interactions.

Encouraging a Thoughtful, Responsible Digital Identity

Creating a positive digital footprint goes beyond avoiding mistakes; it's about building a record of kindness, respect, and responsibility. Parents can remind children that everything they share contributes to their digital identity and encourage them to use online spaces to reflect their values. By strengthening this proactive approach, children develop the skills to manage their online presence in a way that supports their future goals and maintains their self-respect.

A parent and child reviewing privacy settings on a social media app, with a reminder to consider their digital footprint

Digital Citizenship as a Lifelong Skill

Digital citizenship is more than a set of rules; it's a lifelong skill that grows with technology and influences how individuals engage with the world. By teaching values like respect, empathy, and responsibility, parents help children build a foundation for positive online behaviour that will support them in various stages of life—from school and social circles to future careers. Emphasising digital citizenship as a continuous journey encourages children to remain flexible and responsible as they face new digital challenges.

Parents can emphasise that digital citizenship involves both protecting oneself and contributing to safer, healthier online communities. This mindset teaches children to see themselves as active participants in the digital world, responsible for promoting respect and kindness while protecting their own well-being. As children grow and face more complex online interactions, it's important to regularly revisit these principles to support their developing digital identities.

Emma, whose teenage son has been using social media for a few years, encourages him to think about his online actions as part of his legacy. She explains that just as he aims to be kind and responsible in person, his digital behaviour is a reflection of those same values. By viewing digital citizenship as an extension of everyday life, her son has come to appreciate the importance of consistency in both his online and offline interactions.

1. Reinforcing the Importance of Continual Learning

Technology is constantly evolving, and digital citizenship skills need to adapt as well. Parents can encourage children to stay curious about new platforms, tools, and online trends, promoting a mindset of lifelong learning. This approach prepares children to handle emerging digital challenges responsibly, empowering them to stay informed and make choices aligned with their values.

John, whose daughter is interested in new social media trends, encourages her to research each platform's privacy policies and user guidelines before joining. This practice has taught her to evaluate platforms carefully, considering whether they align with her values and privacy preferences. John's encouragement to continually learn about digital spaces has helped his daughter feel more in control and confident as she explores new online communities.

2. Celebrating Positive Digital Contributions

Highlighting children's positive online actions emphasises the idea that digital citizenship is not only about avoiding risks but also about making valuable contributions. Recognising moments when children demonstrate kindness, creativity, or responsibility online encourages them to continue adopting positive habits. This reinforcement helps children see themselves as role models, which can be a motivating factor in maintaining respectful digital behaviour.

Carlos regularly acknowledges his daughter's positive online interactions, such as helping a friend through a difficult time or sharing encouraging comments on social media. By celebrating these actions, Carlos shows his daughter that her kindness matters and impacts others, even in digital spaces. This positive feedback has strengthened her commitment to responsible digital behaviour and has helped her see herself as a supportive presence in her online communities.

3. Building Confidence in Digital Decision-Making

The goal of teaching digital citizenship is to build children's confidence in making wise, responsible choices online. By giving them the tools and guidance to evaluate situations independently, parents empower children to handle complex online interactions with maturity. This confidence prepares them for the varied digital experiences they'll face as they grow, building resilience and flexibility.

Laura, a mother of two, often reminds her children that they have the skills to handle online challenges. Whenever they face something unfamiliar, she encourages them to think through their options, trust their instincts, and remember the values they've discussed as a family. Laura's support has helped her children feel equipped to navigate online spaces with confidence, knowing they can rely on their own judgment to make safe, responsible decisions.

Embracing Digital Citizenship as a Core Family Value

By treating digital citizenship as an ongoing family value, parents create an environment where respect, empathy, and responsibility are integral to their children's online lives. Digital citizenship becomes a natural extension of family values, shaping how children interact with others and view themselves in the digital world. As children adopt these principles, they become not only safe and responsible users but also positive influences on others, contributing to a more respectful and supportive digital community.

ENCOURAGING CRITICAL THINKING ONLINE

The Role of Critical Thinking in Digital Safety

In the fast-paced world of digital media, where information and interactions are constant, critical thinking is an essential skill for children. This ability to evaluate content, question sources, and make reasoned decisions helps children differentiate between reliable information and misleading content, reducing their exposure to potential risks. Critical thinking helps children to approach the digital world with care, creating a foundation for safe, informed online interactions.

Teaching children to think critically isn't about making them sceptical of everything; it's about helping them understand that not all content is equally reliable or trustworthy. This skill is especially valuable when they come across sensational stories, persuasive ads, or rumours on social media. By encouraging curiosity and inquiry, parents can help children become confident, thoughtful digital citizens who make informed decisions.

Laura recently had a discussion with her 11-year-old son about an article he read online claiming an "instant cure" for the common cold. Together, they looked up the claim on a trusted medical website and discovered that the information was misleading. This experience taught Laura's son to question bold claims and use credible resources to verify information, building his understanding of digital content evaluation.

1. Teaching Children to Question What They See Online

Encouraging children to ask questions like "Who created this content?" "Why was it shared?" and "Is there evidence to support this?" helps them approach information with a critical mindset. By asking these questions, children can start to recognise potential biases, identify credible sources, and avoid falling for sensational claims. This process can be practiced through everyday discussions, such as analysing news stories or social media posts together.

Carlos, a father of a teenage daughter, uses current events to teach critical thinking. When they read news stories, he asks her to consider the source's reliability, the purpose of the story, and whether there's enough evidence to support its claims. Over time, this practice has helped her develop a habit of questioning information, which she now applies to other content she encounters online. By teaching her to approach content with a critical eye, Carlos has prepared her to navigate online information responsibly.

2. Recognising Persuasive Tactics and Clickbait

Clickbait headlines and persuasive ads are common on the internet, often designed to capture attention and encourage immediate engagement. Teaching children to recognise these tactics empowers them to make conscious choices about which links to click and which to avoid. Parents can explain that clickbait often prioritises exaggeration over accuracy, encouraging children to look beyond flashy headlines and focus on the actual content.

Emma, whose son is 10, recently introduced him to the concept of clickbait after he clicked on an exaggerated headline about a popular movie. Together, they reviewed the headline and compared it to the actual content, which was less exciting than advertised. This experience helped Emma's son understand that not everything with an eye-catching title is worth his attention, strengthening the importance of looking beyond surface-level appeals.

3. Practicing Safe and Informed Searches

When children conduct online searches, encouraging them to use keywords carefully and check multiple sources for information can improve their research skills. Parents can show children how to identify reputable sources, such as educational websites and official publications, and how to spot unverified or sensational sites. Teaching children to assess search results carefully helps them find trustworthy information, reducing their reliance on potentially misleading sources.

A parent guiding a child through an online search, emphasising source reliability.

James recently taught his teenage son about effective search strategies when researching for a school project. They discussed using specific keywords, comparing information from multiple sources, and verifying facts with credible websites. This guidance has given James's son more confidence in finding reliable information and taught him the importance of being thorough in his online research.

Building Fact-Checking Skills and Emphasising Verification

Fact-checking is a valuable skill that enables children to verify information independently. In an environment where misinformation can spread quickly, the ability to confirm details and assess credibility allows children to make more informed choices about what they believe and share. Fact-checking also helps children develop a habit of thinking critically, making them more resilient to false information and persuasive tactics.

Parents can introduce children to simple fact-checking techniques, such as looking up multiple sources, checking the publication date, and considering the credibility of the author or organisation behind the content. By building these skills early, parents give children the tools to assess content on their own, promoting digital independence and responsibility.

Carlos, who has two children, recently discussed fact-checking with his teenage daughter. After she showed him an article claiming a groundbreaking discovery, they reviewed the source together and checked similar articles on other reputable sites. Through this process, Carlos helped his daughter understand that not all headlines are entirely accurate and that verifying information is key to discerning the truth.

1. Using Fact-Checking Websites and Tools

Several online resources, such as Snopes, FactCheck.org, and Google Fact Check Explorer, are dedicated to verifying news, claims, and rumours. Teaching children to use these tools can make fact-checking an accessible part of their digital habits. Parents can guide children in using these sites, showing them how to look up claims, read through fact-check summaries, and draw conclusions from verified information.

Laura introduced her teenage son to Snopes after he mentioned a viral story that seemed too good to be true. They looked up the claim together, discovering that it was based on an exaggerated rumour. This experience gave Laura's son a hands-on understanding of fact-checking, showing him that reliable information is accessible with just a few extra steps. Now, he feels confident verifying content himself, knowing he has resources to rely on when something feels off.

Parent and child using a fact-checking tool together on a laptop

2. Encouraging Cross-Referencing of Sources

Another effective fact-checking strategy is cross-referencing information across multiple reliable sources. By comparing content from different sites or platforms, children can see if a claim is widely supported or if it seems limited to less reliable sources. This process teaches children that credible information often comes from an agreement of trustworthy sources, while unverified information may lack similar support.

John, whose daughter is in high school, often encourages her to cross-reference sources when researching for projects. He explained that reliable sources, such as trusted news outlets, schools, and official publications, usually agree on the facts. By using this approach, John's daughter has learned to identify reliable sources and avoid unverified claims, building confidence in her research skills.

3. Practicing "Reverse Image Search" for Visual Content

Visual content, such as photos or infographics, is common online, but not all images are genuine or accurately represented. Reverse image search tools, like Google Images or TinEye, allow users to trace images back to their original source. Teaching children how to do a reverse image search can help them verify the authenticity of visual content, making it less likely they'll be misled by edited or deceptive images.

Emma, whose 13-year-old son recently came across a striking photo online, taught him how to use Google's reverse image search. Together, they discovered that the image had been edited to exaggerate certain details, which helped him understand that visuals can be manipulated to convey false information. This experience showed Emma's son the importance of verifying visual content, emphasising that not all images can be taken at face value.

4. Reinforcing the "Think Before You Share" Principle

Encouraging children to fact-check information before sharing it with friends or on social media helps them develop a mindful approach to online interactions. Reminding them to pause and verify before posting promotes responsibility and helps ensure they share accurate information instead of unintentionally spreading rumours or falsehoods.

Laura recently reminded her teenage daughter of the "Think Before You Share" principle after she almost reposted an unverified story. Together, they reviewed the article and found inconsistencies, leading her daughter to decide against sharing it. This approach has made her daughter more careful about what she shares, strengthening the importance of responsibility in her digital presence.

Understanding Ads and Persuasive Tactics

Children are frequently exposed to online advertisements, which are often designed to capture attention quickly and encourage impulse responses. Teaching children to recognise persuasive tactics used in ads helps them make informed choices and resist unnecessary purchases or actions. By understanding the techniques used in digital marketing, children become more aware of the influence ads can have, empowering them to make decisions based on their own needs and values rather than external pressures.

Parents can explain that ads often appeal to emotions, create urgency, or promise inflated benefits to trigger immediate interest. By helping children identify these strategies, parents give them tools to engage with ads thoughtfully and avoid falling for misleading or manipulative tactics.

Carlos recently discussed advertising tactics with his 12-year-old daughter after she expressed interest in a product advertised online. He explained that some ads use phrases like "limited time offer" or "best deal ever" to make people feel they have to act immediately. Carlos encouraged her to take time to think about the product and consider whether she truly needed it. This approach helped his daughter recognise the importance of resisting impulsive decisions, building her awareness of advertising influences.

1. Identifying Common Advertising Techniques

Teaching children to identify techniques like emotional appeal, bandwagon effects, and scarcity can improve their ability to analyse ads critically. Emotional appeal involves triggering specific feelings, like excitement or fear, to prompt a response. The bandwagon effect encourages viewers to join in because "everyone else is doing it," while scarcity creates a sense of urgency by suggesting that opportunities are limited.

Emma recently her son to these techniques after he expressed interest in a product that "everyone is using." She explained that advertisers often exaggerate popularity to increase demand and that "everyone" isn't always accurate. This conversation helped her son realise that his interest in the product was influenced by persuasive language rather than a genuine need, making him more cautious of similar tactics in the future.

2. Teaching the Importance of Researching Products

Encouraging children to research products or services before deciding can help them separate genuine needs from marketing influences. Parents can suggest that children read reviews, compare options, and evaluate products based on quality rather than flashy ads. This approach reinforces the value of making informed choices, teaching children to prioritise substance over style.

Laura's teenage daughter recently wanted to buy a skincare product she saw in an ad. Laura encouraged her to look up reviews from reputable sources and check if the product was suitable for her skin type. Through this research, her daughter discovered that the product didn't have positive reviews and decided against purchasing it. This experience helped her understand the value of research, empowering her to make more informed choices when considering online ads.

3. Practicing "Pause and Reflect" with Ads

One of the simplest strategies for handling online ads is to practice "pause and reflect." This approach involves encouraging children to take a moment to consider whether they really need or want something before acting on an ad's message. By creating a brief pause, children can step back from the immediate influence of persuasive language and evaluate their own feelings about the product.

Carlos introduced a "pause and reflect" approach with his son, who often wanted digital game items advertised online. They agreed to wait a day before making purchases to decide if it was a genuine interest. Over time, his son learned to differentiate between valuable items and temporary desires, becoming more mindful of his spending.

4. Recognising Sponsored Content and Influencer Marketing

Many ads are integrated into content created by influencers or sponsored posts, which can be less obvious than traditional ads. Teaching children to recognise sponsored content helps them understand that influencers may be paid to promote certain products, which may or may not reflect the influencer's genuine opinion. Parents can explain that sponsored content is often labelled as "ad," "sponsored," or "paid partnership," encouraging children to think critically about these endorsements.

Emma recently noticed her teenage daughter following a popular influencer who frequently promoted skincare products. They discussed how influencers might be paid to endorse products, even if they wouldn't personally use them. This conversation helped her daughter understand that while she might enjoy the influencer's content, not every product recommendation was entirely genuine. By learning to identify sponsored content, Emma's daughter has become more discerning about influencer marketing.

Developing a Critical Approach to Online Ads

By learning to identify advertising tactics and approaching ads with a healthy scepticism, children build resilience against impulsive purchases and develop a greater sense of control over their online interactions. Parents can encourage children to prioritise their own needs and values over persuasive messages, reinforcing a mindful approach to digital spaces.

Balancing Online Content with Offline Experiences

With online content available 24/7, balancing digital and offline activities is key for children's well-being. Excessive screen time can reduce their involvement in physical activities, family time, and hobbies that promote a balanced lifestyle. Encouraging offline experiences helps children develop a range of interests, strengthen social skills, and build healthy habits that support both their physical and mental health.

Parents can promote balance by setting aside specific times for screen-free activities, such as family meals, outdoor play, or creative hobbies. By prioritising offline moments, children learn that while the digital world has much to offer, real-life connections and experiences are just as important, if not more so.

Emma, whose son is 10, recently established a "no screens after dinner" rule for their family. They use this time to play board games, read, or simply chat about their day. This routine has become a cherished part of their evening, allowing Emma's son to unwind and focus on connecting with his family. By creating screen-free moments, Emma has helped her son appreciate the value of balance and enjoy the benefits of offline time.

1. Introducing "Digital Detox" Days

A "digital detox" involves intentionally setting aside time to disconnect from digital devices, focusing on activities that don't involve screens. Digital detox days—whether weekly or monthly—give children a chance to reset and re-engage with their physical environment. This practice helps them develop self-awareness around screen use and reminds them of the joy of offline activities.

Carlos recently introduced monthly "digital detox" days in his family. On these days, they go hiking, cook meals together, and enjoy outdoor games, with phones and tablets left at home. His children have come to look forward to these days, which offer a refreshing change from their usual screen-based routines. Through these detox days, Carlos's family has discovered new hobbies and strengthened their bonds, creating lasting memories beyond the digital world.

2. Encouraging Physical Activities and Creative Hobbies

Physical and creative activities not only reduce screen time but also contribute to children's physical and emotional well-being. Engaging in sports, art, music, or other hobbies provides a healthy outlet for self-expression and can help children develop skills that enhance their confidence and self-esteem. Parents can encourage children to explore various offline activities, allowing them to find interests that bring joy and fulfilment outside of screens.

Laura noticed that her teenage daughter spent a lot of time online and wanted to encourage more offline engagement. Together, they tried several creative activities, such as painting and playing musical instruments, until her daughter discovered a passion for photography. Now, they often go on weekend photo excursions, capturing nature and local sights. This new hobby has become a meaningful offline pursuit for Laura's daughter, giving her a sense of achievement and an alternative to screen-based entertainment.

3. *Promoting Outdoor Time and Nature Exploration*

Spending time in nature has been shown to improve mental health, reduce stress, and boost creativity. Encouraging children to explore the outdoors—whether by visiting a local park, going for a hike, or playing outdoor games—helps them connect with the environment and appreciate life beyond screens. Parents can create outdoor routines, like weekend nature walks or family picnics, to foster a love for the natural world.

Emma's family has a tradition of Saturday morning nature walks, where they explore nearby trails and take turns identifying plants and animals. These outdoor excursions have not only provided a screen-free experience but have also increased Emma's children's connection with nature. Through these adventures, they've learned to value outdoor time, finding enjoyment in the simple pleasures of fresh air and open spaces.

4. *Setting an Example of Balanced Digital Use*

Children often mirror their parents' habits, making it important for parents to model balanced screen use. By setting an example—such as limiting phone use during meals, prioritising family activities over digital engagement, and practicing self-care—parents show children that balance is a shared family value. This approach emphasises that while digital tools are useful, real-life interactions and personal well-being come first.

John noticed that his daughter was more likely to put down her phone during meals when he did the same. By trying to keep his phone away and engage in conversation, John demonstrated that family time takes priority. Over time, his daughter has come to value these screen-free meals, recognising the importance of being present with loved ones. This shared commitment to balance has strengthened their relationship and created a positive family culture around digital use.

Embracing a Balanced, Fulfilled Lifestyle

Encouraging a balance between online and offline activities helps children develop a more holistic view of life, where technology is just one part of their experience. Encouraging activities like sports, hobbies, and spending time outdoors helps parents support their children's physical and mental health and happiness while helping them enjoy real-world connections.

Family enjoying outdoor activities together showing the benefits of screen-free time

Critical Thinking as a Lifelong Digital Skill

Critical thinking isn't just a tool for managing screen time or avoiding misinformation; it's a lifelong skill that shapes how children engage with the world, online and offline. Encouraging curiosity, critical thinking, and careful decision-making helps parents prepare children to confidently and independently handle the ever-changing digital world. Promoting critical thinking from a young age helps children build resilience to digital influences, ensuring they can evaluate information, manage risks, and make responsible choices throughout their lives.

As technology continues to evolve, children will face new platforms, persuasive tactics, and content types. With a foundation of critical thinking, they'll be better equipped to adapt to these changes, staying true to their values and maintaining control over their digital interactions. Parents can strengthen the importance of critical thinking by modelling these skills, engaging in open conversations, and supporting children in developing their own sense of judgment.

Emma, whose teenage son has shown great improvement in managing his screen time, often reminds him that critical thinking is a skill he'll use beyond the digital world. She encourages him to ask questions, stay curious, and make decisions based on facts rather than emotions. This perspective has helped her son see critical thinking as a valuable life skill that applies to all areas of his life, giving him confidence in his ability to navigate both online and offline challenges.

1. Reinforcing Mindful Digital Habits

Teaching children to approach the digital world mindfully encourages them to use technology with purpose and awareness. Parents can strengthen habits like fact-checking, questioning sources, and setting boundaries around screen time, helping children view technology as a tool rather than a distraction. By encouraging mindful digital habits, parents help children use technology responsibly, ensuring it enhances rather than detracts from their overall well-being.

Carlos, who regularly discusses digital safety with his teenage daughter, has emphasised the importance of mindful technology use. They often review her digital habits together, identifying areas where she can make small adjustments for a healthier balance. These conversations have empowered her to set her own boundaries and view her screen time choices as part of her personal well-being, building a lifelong habit of self-regulation.

2. Encouraging Adaptability in a Changing Digital Landscape

The digital world is constantly changing, with new trends, tools, and platforms emerging regularly. By encouraging adaptability and a willingness to learn, parents prepare children to handle these changes thoughtfully. Teaching children to stay curious and flexible in their approach to technology helps them stay informed, make wise choices, and maintain control over their digital lives.

Laura, whose teenage son is interested in technology, often encourages him to research new platforms and digital tools. They talk about the benefits and risks of each platform, emphasising that learning about technology is an ongoing process. This approach has helped Laura's son become adaptable, enabling him to explore new digital spaces with confidence and awareness.

3. Celebrating Responsible Digital Choices

Recognising children's responsible digital behaviour reinforces positive habits and motivates them to continue practicing critical thinking. Whether it's managing screen time effectively, verifying information before sharing, or choosing offline activities over screens, celebrating these moments helps children see the value of their efforts. This positive reinforcement strengthens their commitment to responsible digital citizenship and encourages them to embrace critical thinking as an ongoing practice.

John regularly acknowledges his teenage daughter's positive digital choices, like limiting screen time or fact-checking content before sharing. By celebrating these actions, he shows his commitment to responsible technology use and boosts her confidence in making wise decisions. This positive reinforcement has strengthened her independence and encouraged critical thinking in all areas of her life.

Embracing Critical Thinking as a Core Value

By integrating critical thinking as a core family value, parents lay the foundation for a thoughtful, informed approach to the digital world. Children who learn to evaluate content, set boundaries, and balance digital with real-life activities develop a healthier, more fulfilling relationship with technology. These skills, encouraged from an early age, ensure that children can adapt to future digital trends responsibly, equipped to face any new challenges that come their way.

STAYING CURRENT IN THE DIGITAL WORLD

The Importance of Staying Current in Digital Trends

In today's rapidly changing digital world, it's important for both parents and children to stay informed about new technologies, social platforms, and online safety. Being proactive about learning digital trends helps parents anticipate potential risks, understand their children's online interests, and respond to changes in a supportive, informed way. By staying updated on digital developments, parents can empower their children to engage safely and responsibly in an ever-changing online world.

Keeping up with new digital trends doesn't require expert knowledge—just curiosity and a willingness to understand the online experiences that influence children's lives. By following reliable resources on online safety, technology updates, and parenting in the digital age, parents can stay informed about emerging challenges and opportunities. This understanding helps parents have meaningful conversations about digital habits, ensuring family values align with children's online activities.

Carlos, a father of two tech-savvy teens, stays informed about digital safety and trending apps through monthly updates. This helps him engage with his children's online activities, providing support without judgment. His interest in their platforms fosters trust, encouraging open conversations about their digital experiences.

1. Exploring Digital Resources and Parenting Guides

There are several resources available to help parents stay informed about online safety and digital trends. Websites like Common Sense Media, Family Online Safety Institute, and the National PTA offer insights on popular apps, games, and safety tips. Parents can also subscribe to newsletters from reputable sources to receive regular updates. These resources provide reliable, accessible information that empowers parents to make well-informed decisions.

Laura, who has a pre-teen interested in social media, subscribes to a few online safety newsletters. Recently, she received an update about privacy risks associated with a popular messaging app. By discussing these concerns with her daughter and exploring safer alternatives, Laura demonstrated that staying informed helps them make choices that prioritise safety and privacy. This proactive approach has made her daughter feel valued, knowing that her interests are supported responsibly.

2. Staying Aware of Platform Privacy Policies and Updates

Social media platforms, gaming networks, and apps often update their privacy policies, terms of service, or features, affecting the user experience and safety. Parents who stay aware of these changes can guide their children on best practices for privacy, such as adjusting settings to limit data sharing or managing friend requests carefully. Reviewing privacy policies regularly together can help children understand how to use platforms securely.

Emma regularly checks the privacy settings on her children's favourite apps, especially after updates. She uses these opportunities to review each app's features and settings with her children, reinforcing the importance of privacy. Recently, she discovered that one app had changed its default settings to make user profiles more public, so they adjusted the settings to restrict visibility. Emma's commitment to monitoring these updates has helped her children feel confident in protecting their privacy online.

Parent and child reviewing a popular app's privacy settings together

Using Open Discussions to Create a Supportive Digital Environment

Staying informed about digital trends is not only about understanding technology; it's also about creating an open, judgment-free space where children feel comfortable sharing their online experiences. When parents are approachable and willing to learn from their children, they encourage a supportive environment where discussions about digital safety, new apps, or online challenges can happen naturally. This openness strengthens trust, enabling children to seek guidance when needed and reinforcing the idea that exploring the digital world is a shared family effort.

Parents can encourage open discussions by asking about the apps and games their children enjoy, showing genuine interest in how they use their devices, and discussing any challenges or confusing situations they may face online. These talks help parents understand their children's online activities, making it easier to provide the right support. In turn, children see their parents as partners in navigating the digital world, building trust and understanding.

Carlos, for example, frequently asks his teenage daughter about the latest trends on social media. By showing curiosity rather than criticism, Carlos creates a space where his daughter feels comfortable discussing both positive and challenging experiences online. This openness has led to honest conversations about peer pressure, privacy, and online behaviour, allowing Carlos to support his daughter in a way that respects her independence while strengthening family values.

1. Encouraging Children to Share Their Experiences

Creating a habit of sharing online experiences helps children develop self-awareness and feel safe discussing anything that might make them uncomfortable. Parents can ask about recent interactions, new apps, or even funny moments they've faced online. These simple conversations build a foundation of openness, making children more likely to reach out if they come across difficult situations or need advice.

Emma makes it a habit to ask her 11-year-old son about his favourite online games and what he enjoys about them. Through these conversations, she's learned about the challenges he faces, such as handling competitive environments or dealing with other players. This habit has made Emma's son feel more comfortable sharing, knowing that she understands his interests and is there to support him when he encounters tricky situations online.

2. Demonstrating a Willingness to Learn Together

When parents show a willingness to learn about new technologies or platforms alongside their children, it builds a sense of partnership. This approach supports the idea that digital navigation is a family effort, where both parents and children grow their understanding together. Parents can ask their children to explain new apps or trends, showing that they value their children's knowledge and experiences, which promotes mutual respect and collaboration.

Laura, whose teenage daughter recently started using a new social media app, asked her daughter to show her how it works. They explored the app's features together, discussing privacy settings, content types, and how her daughter felt about using the platform. By learning about the app together, Laura showed her daughter that she valued her input, helping her feel respected and supported. This shared experience created a stronger bond, making her daughter more open to future discussions about online safety and privacy.

3. Reinforcing the Value of Independent Research

Encouraging children to research their own questions about online safety and privacy instils a sense of responsibility. Parents can guide children to trusted resources, teaching them how to find reliable information on their own. This skill prepares children to face future digital challenges and encourages them to take responsibility for their own online safety.

Carlos recently encouraged his teenage son to research privacy settings for a gaming platform. They reviewed his findings together, discussing which settings offered the best protection and how to apply them. This exercise taught Carlos's son the importance of staying informed and reminded him that he has the ability to safeguard his own online experiences. By encouraging independent research, Carlos instilled a sense of responsibility in his son, helping him gain confidence to make informed choices online.

4. Setting an Example of Continuous Learning

Children often mirror the behaviours of the adults around them. When parents make an effort to stay informed and adapt to new digital developments, they set an example of responsible digital citizenship. By openly sharing what they learn about online safety or privacy updates, parents demonstrate that digital learning is a lifelong process, one that can be embraced with curiosity and adaptability.

Emma frequently shares new insights about digital safety with her children, whether it's a recent privacy update or a new trend in digital tools. By discussing her own learning process, Emma encourages her children to stay engaged in their own digital safety practices. This approach shows them that digital responsibility is something they can practice throughout their lives, strengthening the importance of adaptability and staying informed.

Creating a Lasting Culture of Digital Awareness

Open discussions, active learning, and shared digital experiences help build a lasting culture of awareness within the family. When children feel involved in these conversations and see that their input is valued, they're more likely to take ownership of their digital safety and develop a proactive approach to new technologies. This culture of openness and curiosity provides a strong foundation, helping children approach future digital experiences with confidence and awareness.

Identifying Reliable Resources and Assessing Digital Safety Trends

In the expansive digital world, it's important for parents to use credible resources to stay informed about online safety and technology trends. Knowing where to find trustworthy information allows parents to guide their children effectively and respond to new digital challenges with confidence. By focusing on reliable sources, parents can avoid sensationalised information and instead rely on evidence-based guidance that supports safe, responsible digital habits.

Parents can assess the credibility of a resource by considering its source, purpose, and track record. Trusted organisations like Common Sense Media, the Family Online Safety Institute, and educational institutions offer up-to-date, reliable information. These sources often publish expert articles, research studies, and guides tailored to parents, providing a balanced perspective on digital topics relevant to family life. Additionally, staying informed about key trends, such as emerging social media apps or changes in privacy laws, allows parents to anticipate and address issues before they become significant concerns.

Carlos regularly checks Common Sense Media for updates on popular apps and games, using its detailed reviews and safety tips to guide conversations with his children. By relying on a reputable resource, Carlos ensures that his guidance is well-informed and based on expert advice, helping his children navigate their favourite digital platforms responsibly.

Family discussing a new app or digital trend together, emphasising openness and learning

1. Verifying the Source's Credibility

When researching digital safety information, it's important to verify the credibility of the source. Parents should ensure the resource is linked to a reputable organisation, authored by experts in technology or child development, and free from exaggerated or biased content. Relying on evidence-based sources ensures that parents are equipped with accurate, helpful information that truly benefits their children's safety and well-being.

Emma recently came across an article about screen time recommendations and wanted to ensure its credibility before discussing it with her children. She verified that the article was published by a respected paediatric association, giving her confidence that the advice was research-based and aligned with expert recommendations. By using credible sources, Emma set a high standard for her family's digital learning, ensuring that they rely on accurate, unbiased information.

2. Watching for Bias and Evaluating Purpose

Assessing the purpose of a digital resource helps parents identify any potential bias, which may influence the information presented. Resources created for educational purposes often prioritise balanced, research-backed insights, while content from commercial sources may emphasise specific products or viewpoints. By considering the purpose behind the content, parents can make informed choices about which resources best support their family's digital needs.

Laura, who frequently researches digital trends, noticed that some online articles she read promoted specific products or apps. She explained to her children that certain websites may have commercial interests, encouraging them to assess content critically. This conversation emphasised the importance of balanced information, helping Laura's children understand that not all online content has the same level of objectivity. Laura's approach taught her children to think critically about the information they encounter, promoting a habit of careful evaluation.

3. Reviewing Safety and Privacy Updates Regularly

Digital platforms frequently update their features, privacy settings, and policies to adapt to changing technology and regulations. Parents who review these updates regularly are better prepared to adjust their family's digital safety settings as needed. Many platforms, such as social media apps and gaming networks, offer newsletters or update notifications that inform users about new privacy options and features, making it easier to stay informed.

Carlos recently received a notification about new privacy settings on his teenage son's favourite gaming platform. By reviewing the update together, they discussed the importance of adjusting settings to protect personal information. This proactive approach helped Carlos's son understand that staying safe online requires regular attention, and it gave him confidence in managing his own privacy. By staying informed about platform updates, Carlos strengthened the importance of ongoing digital safety.

4. *Following Digital Safety Organisations and Experts*

Many digital safety organisations and experts provide valuable insights through blogs, social media, and online forums. Following reputable experts allows parents to receive timely information on trends, challenges, and tips, often adapted to specific age groups or types of platforms. Parents can create a curated list of reliable resources, making it easy to stay updated without feeling overwhelmed by the volume of information available.

Emma follows child safety organisations on social media to stay updated on online safety trends, screen time tips, and new apps. These expert-backed updates help her stay informed and share relevant advice with her family, enabling her to address new concerns promptly.

Creating a Personalised Family Safety Strategy

By identifying reliable resources and staying informed about key digital trends, parents can create a personalised approach to digital safety that meets their family's unique needs. This proactive approach helps children confidently explore the digital world, with parents providing informed guidance and support. A personalised approach to safety helps families remain flexible, prepared, and resilient in an ever-changing digital world.

Creating a Proactive Family Media Plan

A family media plan is an effective way to maintain balance, set boundaries, and manage new digital trends in a structured and flexible manner. By setting clear guidelines on screen time, online behaviour, and privacy, parents can encourage purposeful use of digital devices at home. A proactive plan also encourages children to take part in shaping their own digital habits, making them feel responsible for their choices. Regularly revisiting the plan allows the family to adapt to new apps, games, and online activities as they emerge.

An effective media plan covers a range of areas, such as screen time limits, acceptable content, privacy settings, and device-free zones. By setting expectations in advance, parents establish a shared understanding of the role technology plays within the family. Children who participate in creating these guidelines are more likely to respect and follow them, as they feel a sense of ownership over the rules. A family media plan is not static; it evolves with each child's age, maturity, and interests, providing a flexible foundation that grows alongside the family's digital needs.

Carlos and his family have a media plan that they review every six months. They use this time to discuss what's working, adjust screen time limits, and consider new digital interests. Recently, his teenage daughter wanted to join a new social media platform, so they added guidelines for responsible use of social media to their plan. By involving his daughter in the planning process, Carlos helped her feel responsible for her online behaviour, reinforcing a shared commitment to digital safety.

1. Setting Clear Guidelines on Screen Time

Screen time is a common concern for families, so it's important to set limits that suit each child's age and daily schedule. A family media plan can set clear screen time limits for school days and weekends, helping children balance online activities with homework, family time, and other responsibilities. Establishing these boundaries ahead of time helps avoid daily conflicts and provides a predictable structure for children to follow.

Emma, who has two children with different screen time needs, set up specific guidelines in their family media plan. Her 8-year-old has a daily limit of one hour, while her teenager has a flexible limit based on school assignments and extracurricular activities. This structured approach has minimised disagreements and helped both children understand that screen time is a privilege they need to manage responsibly. By customising screen time rules, Emma has created a balanced approach that meets each child's needs.

2. Defining Device-Free Zones and Times

Device-free zones, such as family meals, bedrooms, and study areas, create dedicated spaces where children can disconnect from screens and focus on in-person interactions or restful activities. A family media plan can also specify device-free times, like during meals or before bedtime, helping children develop routines that support their overall well-being. These boundaries emphasise the importance of mindfulness and quality time, showing children that real-life connections take priority.

Laura's family has a simple rule: no devices at the dinner table. This practice encourages open conversations, where everyone shares highlights from their day. Recently, they added bedrooms as device-free zones, ensuring that sleep remains a priority. Laura's children appreciate this structure, and it has helped them enjoy more meaningful family moments. By including these boundaries in their media plan, Laura has shown her children that technology should enhance their lives, not disrupt it.

3. Establishing Privacy and Safety Practices

A family media plan can include specific guidelines for privacy settings, appropriate online interactions, and reporting suspicious content. By addressing these areas in the plan, parents equip children with a toolkit of safety practices they can apply as they explore the digital world. Reviewing privacy settings together ensures that children understand the importance of protecting their personal information, and discussing safe online behaviour reinforces a respectful approach to digital interactions.

Carlos's media plan includes regular check-ins on privacy settings for his children's devices. They review who can see their profiles, adjust friend lists, and discuss the importance of avoiding risky interactions online. By establishing these practices as part of their plan, Carlos has created a culture of digital responsibility that his children embrace. This proactive approach makes privacy and safety habits second nature, empowering his children to protect themselves online.

4. Incorporating Guidelines for New Apps and Platforms

As children grow, their digital interests increase, leading them to explore new apps, games, and platforms. A family media plan that includes guidelines for adopting new digital experiences encourages children to be mindful about their choices. Parents and children can discuss potential risks, review privacy options, and decide whether a new platform supports family values before it's included into their routines.

Emma's teenage son recently expressed interest in using a popular messaging app. Together, they researched the app's privacy features, reviewed its terms of use, and decided on a few safety guidelines before allowing him to join. This approach helped him understand that digital decisions require thoughtful consideration. Including this process in their media plan helped Emma take a proactive approach to new technology, teaching her son to assess digital tools responsibly and thoughtfully.

Reviewing and Adapting the Media Plan Regularly

As children mature and digital trends evolve, a family media plan benefits from regular reviews and adjustments. Revisiting the plan together allows families to celebrate positive digital habits, address any concerns, and update guidelines as needed. By keeping the plan flexible, parents show that they respect their children's growth and independence, creating a supportive environment where digital habits can develop responsibly.

The Long-Term Benefits of a Family Media Plan

A well-maintained family media plan does more than set boundaries; it nurtures lifelong habits that support responsible, balanced technology use. By creating a structured approach to digital habits, the media plan provides children with a framework for managing their time, maintaining privacy, and making safe choices as they grow. This sense of structure reinforces the idea that technology should serve a positive purpose in their lives, encouraging children to be intentional in their online interactions and mindful of their time.

Involving children in creating and updating the family media plan helps them understand digital habits and family rules. This participation boosts their confidence, teaches responsibility, and allows them to set limits collaboratively. As they grow, these lessons guide them in making responsible online choices.

Family sitting together, reviewing a media plan that outlines screen time, device-free zones

1. Fostering Digital Balance and Healthy Habits

The family media plan's emphasis on balance ensures that children experience the benefits of both digital and offline activities. Creating screen-free spaces, prioritising face-to-face interactions, and encouraging outdoor or creative activities help promote a balanced and healthy lifestyle. Children learn to see technology as a tool, not a dependency, building a foundation for a healthy relationship with digital devices.

Emma's children, who enjoy their family's designated device-free times, have grown to appreciate these moments as opportunities to bond, explore hobbies, or simply relax without screens. Over time, they have internalised this balance, seeing digital devices as one part of their lives rather than the main focus. By strengthening healthy habits, Emma's media plan has helped her children develop a balanced, fulfilling lifestyle that they carry with them outside the home.

2. Encouraging Responsible Digital Citizenship

By addressing privacy settings, online behaviour, and safety practices, a family media plan supports children in becoming respectful, responsible digital citizens. They learn that their online actions have consequences and that maintaining privacy is essential for staying safe. This understanding helps children respect themselves and others, encouraging them to use digital spaces in line with family values.

Laura's teenage son has become more mindful of his online presence, understanding that his actions reflect both his values and his family's. The family media plan's guidelines on responsible sharing, privacy, and respectful communication have helped him approach online interactions with greater care. This awareness has enhanced his digital citizenship, enabling him to make choices that positively impact his online communities.

3. Reinforcing Independence Through Structure

A family media plan provides a structured yet flexible framework that encourages independence. As children demonstrate responsibility, parents can gradually adjust the plan, giving them more freedom while reinforcing trust. This gradual approach shows children that responsible choices lead to increased independence, fostering a healthy sense of autonomy.

Carlos and his family regularly revisit their media plan to reflect each child's growth and changing needs. For his older son, this meant extending screen time for academic projects and trusted social platforms. By adapting the plan to his children's maturity, Carlos has shown that independence comes with responsibility, helping his children feel empowered and respected. This structure has built their confidence and prepared them to make safe, independent choices as they gain more online freedom.

4. Building a Lifelong Foundation for Digital Well-Being

The habits and values established through a family media plan become a foundation for lifelong digital well-being. Children who grow up with clear boundaries, respectful communication, and a balanced approach to technology are better equipped to handle future digital challenges. As technology continues to evolve, these principles serve as a steady guide, supporting children in making choices that enhance their lives without compromising their values.

Emma's teenage daughter has taken the lessons from their media plan to heart, demonstrating balanced digital habits even as she gains independence. She's learned to prioritise face-to-face connections, set boundaries around screen time, and approach new apps responsibly. This foundation has prepared her for the future, equipping her with the tools to navigate an increasingly digital world with confidence and self-respect.

Celebrating Digital Successes Together

A family media plan is an ongoing journey, one that celebrates growth, responsibility, and family connection. By involving children in setting and updating guidelines, parents create a shared commitment to digital well-being. Each positive choice, responsible interaction, and mindful screen habit strengthens the family's values, building a legacy of healthy, thoughtful technology use that children carry into adulthood.

CONCLUSION

In today's digital world, raising children with a strong foundation in online safety, critical thinking, and responsible digital citizenship is both a challenge and a responsibility. As parents, teachers, and caregivers, our role is to guide children through the challenges of technology while equipping them with the skills and awareness to navigate digital spaces safely and responsibly on their own. This book has explored practical strategies for open communication, clear guidelines, parental controls, monitoring, digital citizenship, critical thinking, and continuous learning to help families build a healthy relationship with technology.

By actively engaging in children's digital activities, encouraging open conversations, and setting clear boundaries, we create a supportive environment where they can explore, learn, and connect online with confidence and safety. The family media plan serves as a tool that adapts with children's evolving needs, reinforcing values of balance, respect, and responsibility. Teaching critical thinking and encouraging caution about online content helps children evaluate information and make informed decisions in today's complex digital world.

The journey toward digital safety and responsible online habits is ongoing, evolving as new trends, platforms, and technologies emerge. By remaining informed and open to change, we can continue to support our children as they grow, helping them make wise choices that will serve them throughout their lives. As parents and educators, our commitment to staying engaged, learning, and adapting alongside our children is the foundation of digital resilience.

Finally, this book is a reminder that safe, positive online interactions are possible through guidance, education, and mutual respect. By nurturing these values, we empower the next generation to use technology as a tool for connection, learning, and growth, while safeguarding their well-being and integrity. Together, let's embrace the digital world with confidence and curiosity, ensuring that our children are safe online, strong offline, and equipped for whatever the future holds.

SUMMARY AND KEY POINTS

Chapter 1: The Foundation of Open Communication

- Open communication builds trust, making children feel safe to share online experiences.
- Encourage children to come forward about any discomfort or concerns they encounter online.
- Use real-life examples to discuss online safety, helping them understand potential risks.
- Emphasise that you are a safe resource for guidance on navigating the digital world.

Chapter 2: Setting Clear and Effective Guidelines

- Set specific rules on screen time, device use, and acceptable content.
- Establish structured routines to balance online activities with offline responsibilities.
- Adapt guidelines as children grow to support increasing independence and responsibility.
- Emphasise that guidelines are a family commitment to safety and well-being.

Chapter 3: Mastering Parental Controls and Safety Settings

- Familiarise yourself with parental control tools on devices, apps, and websites.
- Use filters and restrictions to ensure age-appropriate content is accessible.

- Teach children the purpose of these controls, emphasising protection over restriction.
- Regularly review and update settings to align with children's needs and new digital trends.

Chapter 4: Monitoring Online Activity

- Monitor online activity respectfully, balancing privacy and safety.
- Discuss safe online behaviour openly, encouraging children to make responsible choices.
- Use monitoring to guide, rather than control, fostering trust and transparency.
- Adapt monitoring as children mature, shifting from oversight to open dialogue.

Chapter 5: Teaching Digital Citizenship

- Emphasise respect and kindness in online interactions to promote positive digital citizenship.
- Teach children to handle cyberbullying by using reporting and blocking tools.
- Encourage critical thinking when sharing information to prevent spreading misinformation.
- Reinforce the importance of protecting personal information and privacy online.

Chapter 6: Encouraging Critical Thinking Online

- Equip children with tools to evaluate content, including fact-checking and cross-referencing.
- Discuss persuasive tactics in ads, helping them recognise clickbait and emotional appeals.
- Promote balanced screen time by encouraging offline hobbies and outdoor activities.
- Reinforce critical thinking as a lifelong skill that applies beyond the digital world.

Chapter 7: Staying Informed and Updated in the Digital World

- Stay informed about digital trends to engage effectively in children's online lives.

- Create a family media plan that covers screen time, device-free zones, and privacy settings.
- Encourage regular updates to the media plan, reflecting each child's changing needs.
- Model digital resilience and adaptability, showing children that technology is a tool, not a necessity.

A PRACTICAL GUIDE FOR PARENTS TO KEEP KIDS SAFE ONLINE

www.ingramcontent.com/pod-product-compliance
Lightning Source LLC
Chambersburg PA
CBHW071408220526
45469CB00004B/1204